# ENTANGLED TONGUES:
A Short History of the English Language
or The Influence of French on English

# *Praise for* ENTANGLED TONGUES

"Kisch takes a brief look at the building blocks of modern English. Where does the English that is currently spoken come from? Why does it function the way that it does? These are the questions that the author... addresses in this examination of the many different pieces that have come together to form modern English... As hundreds of years of English history are rushed through, the book has many fascinating points to make... All told, the book offers readers different ways of looking at what they say. An edifying account of the evolution of a complex language."
— *Kirkus Reviews*

"Kisch provides a brisk, brief overview of how we got modern English, with a light touch and a focus on the impact of the Norman Conquest on the development of the language. Kisch's survey is inviting, unfussy, and practical, revealing not just the history but... what it all means for us today...

"Fascinating insights abound... Like most of her examples, her explanation of the Bard's use of *thou, thee,* and *you* is inspired and inspiring... this is the kind of enticing introduction to a topic that makes readers want to dig deeper. A helpful bibliography, endnotes for future research, and illustrations ground the history."
— *BookLife: Editor's Pick*

"Carol Williams Kisch traces the influence of the French on the evolution of the English language in this accessible yet scholarly examination... her lively prose, punctuated with anecdotal and humorous commentary, keeps readers engaged... Overall, *Entangled Tongues* offers an enjoyable slice of linguistic history that will be appreciated by students of French or English literature/language and European history enthusiasts alike."
— *Blueink Review*

"*Entangled Tongues: A Short History of the English Language* is a valuable resource for anyone interested in the evolution of the English language... Kisch effectively blends scholarly research with engaging explanations... presents complex linguistic changes in a clear, organized manner that makes the subject approachable without sacrificing depth." — *Midwest Book Review*

"An excellent read. The writing... is... on point, as would be expected in a well-researched book on the history of the English language, but Kisch also makes it accessible to readers like me who are going in pretty green. I learned so much... Overall, this is a great mix of linguistic detail with historical narrative, delivered in a way that enriches understanding for those interested in the evolution of the English language." — *Readers' Favorite: 5 stars*

"*Entangled Tongues* is a lighthearted interrogation of the English language's past. The prose is colloquial and straightforward, and the book's examples are easy to follow. The book includes a bevy of historical and personal anecdotes; they are often humorous, complementing the history sections with their lighthearted tones... A jovial linguistic history text..." — *Foreward Clarion Reviews*

# ENTANGLED TONGUES:
## A Short History of the English Language
### *or* The Influence of French on English

William the Conqueror:
*The Man Who Changed the English Language*

## By Carol Williams Kisch

Copyright © 2025 by Carol M. Williams

All rights reserved. This book may not be reproduced in whole or in part, in any form (beyond that copying permitted by Sections 107 and 108 of the U.S. Copyright Law and except by reviewers for the public press) without written permission from the publisher.

Published by Althof Press, Riverside, California, 2025:
info@althofpress.com

ISBN: 979-8-9999302-0-0
LCCN: 2025917636

Cover Photo: Guillaume-le-Conquérant, Falaise. Peter Robinson/Alamy Stock Photo

Book Cover: Book Cover Designs by C.C.
Title Creation: Housley Literary Services

To my husband, who has brought me along on his journey from no English at all to his current appreciation of Chaucer and Shakespeare, and to our grandchildren.

Also to my teachers: Paul Aubin of Te Awamutu, New Zealand, whose love of history (and Hundred Years War battle tactics!) was contagious and Jean-Louis Ferrier of Paris, France, who insisted that I research Gustave Moreau.

# Preface

This short history of the English language is based on a paper that I wrote for my master's degree. For many years, I used that paper as the basis of my introductory lecture on the first day of classes that I gave for teachers of English, who came from all over the world to study English language teaching methodologies at the University of California.

Since my retirement, I've come back to this subject. When I wrote my original paper, I used only American and British sources. However, for this book, I have also relied on French sources which have not been translated into English, and which present a different and valuable perspective. In addition, I have given extra weight to the conclusions of researchers who bring a competence in both English and French to this topic, as well as an understanding of the language acquisition process.

Information on the evolution of English is, in many areas, abundant and, in other areas, almost non-existent, and the conclusions that historians draw from the available evidence are often contradictory. Therefore, this brief history is simply a glimpse into the multifaceted history of English from the vantage point of one English language teacher. A starting point…

Carol Williams Kisch
August 2025

Medieval English Proverb:

*Jack would be a gentleman if he could speak French.*

# TABLE OF CONTENTS

**Part One:** Making Sense of English Vocabulary, Grammar, and Spelling ................................................. 1

**Part Two:** The Old English Period, 449 to 1066 ......... 9

**Part Three:** The Norman Conquest, 1066 ............... 23

**Part Four:** The Beginning of the End of Old English: The Years after 1066 ......................................... 35

**Part Five:** Middle English: The Hundred Years War and The Black Death ................................................. 45

**Part Six:** The Middle English Period: Richard II, Henry IV, and Henry V/The End of the Hundred Years War ............................................................................ 59

**Part Seven:** A Huge Infusion of French Words into English, 1250 to 1500 ............................................. 73

**Part Eight:** The Power of Old English/ Comet Words ............................................................... 81

**Part Nine:** Phrasal Verbs/The Present Perfect/ The Present Continous/Irregular Verbs ....................... 87

**Part Ten:** Twelve Problems with English Spelling ..... 99

**Part Eleven:** Modern English, 1500 to the Present ..... 109

**Part Twelve:** Conclusion ............................................. 125

Bibliography ................................................................... 131

Endnotes ........................................................................ 135

# PART ONE

MAKING SENSE OF ENGLISH VOCABULARY, GRAMMAR, AND SPELLING

ENTANGLED TONGUES

PART ONE

The **French point of view:** "La langue anglaise n'existe pas. C'est du français mal prononcé." ("The English language doesn't exist. It is badly pronounced French.") Georges Clemenceau, French Prime Minister, 1906-1909, 1917-1920.

**The English point of view:** "So now they have made our English tongue... a hodgepodge of all other speeches." Edmund Spenser, English poet, 1552-1599.

Perhaps you're teaching English or use English every day as a second language. Perhaps you're a native speaker who sometimes wonders about the language that you speak every day, because you've noticed a few things that don't make sense. For example, in Modern English, to express your ability to swim, you say, "Yesterday I could swim, today I can swim, and tomorrow, I ..." Something is missing. I could, I can, ...? What is the future of "I can?" Perhaps you've heard that the English vocabulary is twice as big as the French, German, and other vocabularies (for example, in the largest French dictionary, you have 150,000 entries versus 400,000 in the largest English dictionary).[1] But if all these vocabularies describe a similar world, why is one of these vocabularies, the English vocabulary, so much larger than the others? And finally, who came up with English spelling?

When I was young, I worked in French summer camps, studied in France, and got a degree in French Literature, but I never thought about the relationship between French and English (and German which I speak just a bit) until I taught English and worked as a translator in West Africa. It was only then that I began to think about what a strange language English is. Now, why do I say strange?

**FIRST: ENGLISH VOCABULARY.** As I translated, from French into English, practical information about sick West African cows for the Montana cattle ranchers who had come to help, I noticed that many words in the English-language documents that I created were clearly words of Germanic origin. On the other hand, later in France, as I worked on a team which translated American psychology articles, I noticed that many of the words in the English-language documents were clearly words of French origin...

I started to wonder why so many basic English words, the words that we use every day, such as *come, go, work, play, love, hate*, are so similar to German words. For example, look at this German sentence and see if you can guess the meaning: "Das ist ein gutes Buch." You probably guess that "Das ist ein gutes Buch" means "This is a good book." Or speaking about my family, how about, "Ich habe ein Vater, eine Mutter, eine Schwester, und ein Brüder?" You probably guess that I mean, "I have a father, a mother, a sister, and a brother." Now, listen to what a French astronaut said on French television about the experience of being an astronaut. Can you guess what she is saying? (Just move a few words around.) "C'est une aventure humaine absolument extraordinaire." ("It is an absolutely extraordinary human adventure.") Or, closer to home, how about this? "Carol adore le chocolat." We see that, if you speak English, you can often understand German sentences which express very basic everyday ideas, as well as French sentences which convey more abstract ideas.

I recently saw some research which said that 96 out of the 100 most commonly used English words are Germanic in origin. Then I saw other research which said, no, no, *all* of the 100 most commonly used English words are Germanic. I then saw other studies which said that 39% of the English vocabulary comes from Germanic languages, 41% comes from French, 15% from Latin, and 5% from other languages. Then I saw other research which said, no, no, no, only 25% of all English words come from

PART ONE

Germanic languages. Which percentages are correct? Well, it depends. It depends on how we define the size of the English vocabulary. Do we count the entries in a dictionary? If so, which dictionary? Do *a question*, *to question*, and *a questionnaire* count as one word, two words, or three words? Or do we follow thousands of native speakers for months and count the words that they use? In writing? In speaking? In both? Which people do we follow? Businessmen? Government officials? Talk show hosts? Actors in a popular soap opera?

What do we say about an English word such as *slave* (which comes from the Slavic people of Eastern Europe who were a favorite target of the Viking slave traders)? This word *slave* came from the Viking language Norse into Latin more than 1500 years ago and then migrated from Latin into French, and finally from French into English after the Norman/French Conquest of England. So, from which language did the word *slave* come into English? What about a word like *beer*? It seems equally probable that it came from Latin or from a Germanic language. So, do we count it as a Latin word or a Germanic word? All of these ideas are interesting, but the central question remains: how did the English language acquire such a huge vocabulary?

**SECOND: ENGLISH GRAMMAR**. I noticed that the more often we use an English word, the more likely it is that this word is of Germanic origin and that it is irregular. What do I mean by irregular? I mean that, instead of adding the usual, or regular, *-s* to make a noun plural (for example, one bicycle/two bicycles), we say, "one wife/two wives, one man/two men, one child/two children, one foot/two feet, one fish/two fish," etc. Or, instead of adding the usual, or regular, *-ed* to a verb to indicate the past, we say, "Today I *am*.../Yesterday I *was*.../Recently, I *have been*..." or we say "Today I *go*/Yesterday I *went*... / Recently, I *have gone*..."

In English, I may ask you, "Can you swim?" (from the German *kann*, as in "Kannst du schwimmen?") And you may answer, "Yes, I can." However, what if we want to ask about the future? What is the future of "I can?" Answer: There is no future of "I can" in English. We must switch away from the Germanic *can* to the French *capable* which, with a slightly different pronunciation, becomes *capable* in English. Then we shorten *capable* to *able*, and we say, "Tomorrow I will be able to swim." Hmmm. Strange.

**THIRD: ENGLISH SPELLING.** In the United Sates, many young students have the experience of participating in spelling competitions which we call spelling bees. We even have a national spelling bee in Washington D.C. every year where we celebrate students from all over the U.S. because… they can spell English words! But this is unthinkable in many other countries. I have often heard, "In my language, if you can spell it, you can say it and if you can say it, you can spell it!" No spelling bees. So, I started to think about English spelling. I noticed that, in German, for example, you have *ein haus*, h-a-u-s, which, in English, becomes a *house*, h-o-u-s-e. So, *house* is an English word which clearly comes from German, but the spelling feels, and it is…, very French. Hmmm. Strange…

So, I had many questions which I tried to answer when I wrote a paper for my master's degree titled, "The Influence of French on English." I wrote that paper from a standard British/American point of view which (when it does acknowledge the tremendous influence of French on English*) tends to see the history of English as a heroic comeback story. That is, as the story of a language which, after the Norman/French invasion of England in 1066, was neglected, mutilated, and could easily have disappeared from the earth, if not for a series of fortuitous historical events which allowed the language to recreate itself and ultimately to produce some of the greatest literature ever written.

PART ONE

However, there is a different point of view, most recently expressed in a fascinating book which was just published in France last year, 2024, titled *"La langue anglaise n'existe pas" C'est du français malprononcé*. (*"The English language doesn't exist." It is badly pronounced French*.) In this book, Bernard Cerquiglini suggests that, after the Norman Conquest of England, the French language offered to the English language some of its own superior vocabulary as a gift, as it were, and that it is only because of this infusion of sophisticated French vocabulary that such a dull, pedestrian language could hope to become the complex, internationally dominant language that it is today. That is, the story of English is essentially the story of its everlasting debt to French. As Cerquiqlini puts it, "Sans les Normands, l'anglais serait aujourd'hui un second néerlandais." ("Without the Normans, English today would be a second Dutch.")

Which point of view best represents the historical and linguistic reality? Let's see what *you* think as we take a look at the history of the English language.

In **Part Two**, we'll go back to the year 449 to see how the English language was born.

---

\* Williams (2004) writes of "the power of the overarching narrative of English history that represses the memory of the 'Norman yoke' altogether." [2]

ENTANGLED TONGUES

# PART TWO

## THE OLD ENGLISH PERIOD, 449 TO 1066

ENTANGLED TONGUES

PART TWO

1. Roman Britain

To understand how *Old English* became *Middle English* and finally the *Modern English* which we speak today, we need to go back in time to the year 449. Where were your ancestors in 449? Well, a few of my ancestors were Celts, living in England and possibly happy that the Roman soldiers who had occupied England for hundreds of years had gone back to Rome, leaving behind only a few Latin words and place names. However, once the Roman soldiers left England undefended, some of my other ancestors saw that there were opportunities for themselves in England.

This time, the invaders were Germanic tribes: Angles (from an area in Denmark which is still called Angeln), Saxons (from an area in Germany which is still called Lower Saxony), and Jutes (from Jutland in what is now Denmark). All three of these groups are often lumped together as *Anglo-Saxons*, and so we will do that, too. In wave after wave, the Anglo-Saxons came over the sea to settle in England and, in turn, many Celts fled north into Scotland, west into Wales, west over the sea to Ireland, or south to Brittany in France. The current consensus seems to be that the Anglo-Saxons took only a very few words, such as *crag* and *bin*, and a few place names, such as *Thames, Avon,* and *London,* from those Celts who remained in England.*

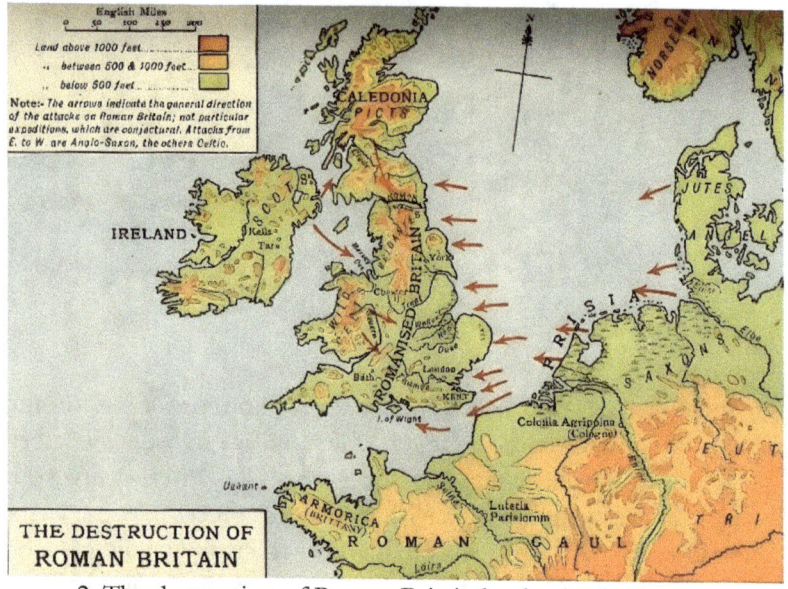

2. The destruction of Roman Britain by the Anglo-Saxons

On a side note, in the summer of 1967, I was at a summer camp in northwestern France, in Brittany, and one day, as I was walking down a country road, I heard farmers speaking to each other in a language that I didn't understand. That language was Breton, the language which their Celtic ancestors had brought to Brittany from England when they fled from the Anglo-Saxons 1500 years ago. Even today, in Brittany, we see the descendants of Celts coming every year, from all over, to celebrate their Celtic identities and languages with a Celtic music festival.

But… back to England in the year 449. As the Celtic tribes fled from them, the Anglo-Saxon tribes began to establish their own territories in England. Each tribe called its dialect "Englisc" and, in fact, the three Anglo-Saxon dialects were very similar. All

PART TWO

3. Anglo-Saxon fashions

of them already included a few Latin words, such as *wine, cup, dish, wall, street, mile,* and *cheap,* which the Anglo-Saxons had learned from the Romans when they traded with them in Germany and Denmark, before the Anglo-Saxons moved to England.

4. Augustine preaching before King Ethelbert, 597 A.D.

In 597, about 150 years after the first Anglo-Saxon invasions, Christian missionaries arrived in England from Italy and added about 450 more Latin words to the Anglo-Saxon dialects, words such as *angel, candle, paper, disciple, history, master, offer, fever, school,* and *silk*. Three years later, we get the first texts written in this *Englisc;* therefore, most linguists give the year 600 as the official birthdate of the English language.

PART TWO

In the late 700s, Vikings from Norway and Denmark began to attack England to rob and plunder. Under Alfred the Great (849-899), the Anglo-Saxons were able to push the Vikings back towards the north and east of England, where they settled down in their own area called the Danelaw. England then had four major Germanic dialects: the Anglo-Saxon dialects (*Anglian, West Saxon* or *Wessex*, and *Kentish*) plus the Viking dialect, which is generally called *Norse,* so we will call it that, too.

5. Viking armada/6. The Viking sails grew to be dreaded

This Norse dialect was very similar to the Anglo-Saxon dialects, differing especially in the inflections that it added to its words.[3]** (We'll discuss inflections in a moment.) As the Anglo-Saxons interacted with their new Viking neighbors, their dialects absorbed about 40 words connected, for the most part, with sailing and raiding.[4] Many more Norse words would come into English a few centuries later, so that, today, we use about 1800 words that come from the Vikings: 1) words such as *want, take, get, give, kid, husband, big,* 2) almost any word that begins with *sk-*, s+uch as *sky, skirt, ski,* and 3) the pronouns: *they, their,* and *them.*[5]

Eventually, the Wessex dialect of Alfred the Great became the dominant dialect in England, the dialect which we call *Old English.* This Wessex, this "Old English," was the language of the English royal court, government, church, and literature until the Norman Conquest. So, what was Old English like? Let's take a little detour from history for a moment to discuss Old English.

7. Britain in 886 A.D.

Old English (or Anglo-Saxon, as some people call it) was a *synthetic* language whereas Modern English, like French, is an *analytic* language. What's the difference, you ask? Well, in an analytic language, we know whether a word is a subject or an object by looking at the position of the word in a sentence. Compare "John ate the lion" and "The lion ate John." These sentences have opposite meanings and so it's of great interest for John to know whether his name is going to come before the verb or after the verb. But no words change. Only the *positions* of the words in each sentence change. As we see, in an analytic language, *word order* determines the meaning of a sentence. Even if we use the passive tense, the order of the words still determines the meaning of the sentence, as in "John was eaten by the lion" versus "The lion was eaten by John."

PART TWO

On the other hand, in a *synthetic* language, like Old English or German today, word order does not determine the meaning of a sentence. Instead, we can put either the subject or the object before the verb without changing the meaning of the sentence. In a synthetic language, it is the *inflections,* that is, the word variations and endings that we attach to nouns, verbs, adjectives, etc. that determine the meaning of a sentence.

I don't speak Old English so here is an example using Modern German. Let's say that we want to translate the sentence, "The young woman gave the old man a glass of water." So, we have the young woman (Die junge Frau), the old man (dem alten Mann), and a glass of water (ein Glas Wasser). We can translate this as "Die junge Frau hat... dem alten Mann... ein Glas Wasser gegeben." However, we can also change the word order and say, "Dem alten Mann... hat die junge Frau... ein Glas Wasser gegeben." The word order changes, but the meaning of the sentences stays the same. Whether we put "die junge Frau" or "dem alten Mann" at the beginning or in the middle of the sentence, the meaning is the same; it is the word endings and word variations, that is, *the inflections,* not the word order, which tell us that the young woman *did* the action and that the old man *received* the action.

Old English, like German today, was full of inflections. Today, however, English has only a few remaining inflections, such as the word endings, *-ed* and *-s*. By adding *-ed* to a verb, we can change the meaning of the verb from the present to the past. By adding an *-s* to a noun, we change the noun from singular to plural. We can also create a comparison by attaching *-er* or *-est* to an adjective, as in *big, bigger,* and *biggest.* In the past, Old English verbs were inflected to show whether the subject was first person, second person, or third person, singular, or plural, etc., while articles, such as *the* and *a,* were inflected to show whether a noun was masculine, feminine, or neuter.

Today, we sometimes have a choice in English whether to use an old Germanic synthetic structure or one of the analytic structures which came into English from French. So, we can discuss *Mozart's* five violin concertos, adding an apostrophe and the inflection *-s* to the word *Mozart* to show possession, or we can discuss the five violin concertos *of Mozart*, using the preposition *of* and word order to show possession.

8. King Alfred found much pleasure in reading

When people look at the basic nature of most of the Old English words that we still use today, such as *good, bad, eat, drink, sleep, sing*, they may imagine that Old English was a simple, primitive language, inadequate for great literature. But, in fact, Old English was a highly resourceful and nuanced language which produced (in part, due to King Alfred the Great) a huge body of literature, including the epic poem *Beowulf.*\*\*\*

Old English was able to create a wide range of images from a single root word. For example, one Old English root word, *mod* (that is, *mood* in Modern English) could mean *courage, boldness, heart,*

PART TWO

*mind, haughtiness,* and *pride*. By attaching prefixes or suffixes to the root word *mod*, Old English created over a hundred additional words, with a wide range of meanings, including *sorrow, high-minded, arrogant, intelligent, bold, folly, kindness, affection, cowardice,* and so on. Some Old English words in *Beowulf* had thirty synonyms! [6] ****

9./10. *Beowulf*

Old English also combined words to describe ordinary things, such as *earrings*, as well as to create new images and concepts. We still do that today in English, but we are as likely to steal word combinations from Modern German as we are to create our own. For example, we may send our children to a *kindergarten* (that is, a children/garden), we may speak of the *shadenfreude* (that is, the harm/joy) that we feel if we're happy to know that our enemy is suffering, or we may discuss the *zeitgeist* (that is, the time/spirit) of the world today.

So, how was English transformed from a synthetic language, with a rich Germanic vocabulary, into an analytic language, with more words of French origin than of Germanic origin?

In **Part Three**, we'll meet the two men whose rivalry transformed the English language forever: Harold Godwinson, the Earl of Wessex, and William, the Duke of Normandy.

11. Harold Godwinson    12. William the Conqueror

\* There is some debate about *how many* Celts left England, *how quickly* they left, and *how violent* the Anglo-Saxon invasion was, as well as the degree of Celtic influence on the Anglo-Saxon dialects. Recent DNA testing of the English population suggests that many more Celts stayed in England and intermarried with the invading Germanic tribes than had been previously thought.

\*\* Old English words and Norse words were so similar that it is often difficult to say whether a Modern English word should be classified as coming from Old English or from Norse.

\*\*\* The French-Canadian historian Serge Lusignan writes (2004), "Au moment de la conquête, l'anglo-saxon avait atteint un haut niveau de développement au plan littéraire, le plus élevé sans doute parmi les langues vernaculaires européennes de l'époque." ("At the time of the Conquest, Anglo-Saxon had reached a high level of literary development, no doubt the highest among the European vernacular languages of the time.")[7]

**** If you're a fan of *The Lord of the Rings* books and movies, you may know that J.R.R. Tolkien translated *Beowulf*, the inspiration for his *Lord of the Rings*, from Old English into Modern English in 1926. However, his translation was not published until 2014.

ENTANGLED TONGUES

# PART THREE

**THE NORMAN CONQUEST, 1066**

ENTANGLED TONGUES

PART THREE

13. William the Conqueror arriving in England

On January 5th, 1066, the childless English king, Edward the Confessor, died. As Edward lay dying, he designated his wife's brother, Harold Godwinson, the powerful Earl of Wessex and the acting king as his successor. After Edward died, the English Witan, composed of the 60 most powerful English earls, immediately met and offered the crown to the respected and highly competent Godwinson, who became King Harold II the next day, January 6th, 1066.

However, across the English Channel, in northern France, William, Duke of Normandy, believed that he should be the next king of England because 1) he was a distant cousin of King Edward on Edward's French mother's side, 2) he claimed that, many years earlier, Edward had promised him the throne, and 3) he also claimed that Harold had once solemnly sworn to support his absolute right to the English throne. (British sources are less likely to believe William's version of these events than French sources are.)

On the morning of September 28th, William's soldiers, horses, and support personnel landed on English beaches, in close to 800 ships and 200 smaller boats,[8] including his own ship, La Mora, a gift from his wife, Mathilde. (Once again, a few of my ancestors invaded England to fight some of my other ancestors who were already living there!) Godwinson was far off, in the north of England, fighting the Viking King of Norway, Harald Hardrada, who thought that *he* should be the new king of England. Godwinson's victory was so complete that this was the last time that the Vikings ever invaded England. But, as Godwinson was celebrating his stunning victory, a messenger arrived to tell him that William's army had landed near Pevensey Bay. Godwinson then hurried south to confront William and on October 14$^{th}$ at the Battle of Hastings, he was killed with (as I learned in Mr. Aubin's 6$^{th}$ form history class in Te Awamutu, New Zealand) an arrow in his right eye.

14. Edith finds Harold on the battlefield

I also learned that his wife, Edith Swan-Neck, searched the battlefield for days until she identified her husband's body and then went to William and demanded that her husband be given a proper burial. A story which, as it turns out, is not totally true, but which I personally like a lot. In any case, it seems that Godwinson's body eventually did get a, more or less, proper

PART THREE

burial. On the other hand, William of Normandy got England. After marching his troops to London, terrorizing towns and villages along the way, William was crowned King William I of England on Christmas Day, 1066.

Now, the new King William knew that the English people did not want him to be their king. He also faced another problem: his own Norman army did not have the resources to conquer England. So, he had been obliged to get men, ships, and horses from other French nobles, by promising to give them land and positions in England if he won. Now he needed to keep his promises. What to do? An obvious answer was to eliminate the entire landowning English upper class, which he did. The twelve English earls were all killed, either at the Battle of Hastings or elsewhere, and their lands and positions were distributed to men who had fought with William. William also rewarded many of his supporters with the lands of the lower English nobility and lesser landowners who had been killed or who had fled to the European continent. And so, twenty years after the Conquest, in 1086, the upper class in England was a Norman-French upper class, with only two of the Anglo-Saxon lords remaining: Colswein of Lincoln and Thurkill of Arden.[9]

In addition, almost all of the English clergy were replaced by Norman bishops, abbots, priests, and monks. Only one bishop, the respected Wulfstan, Bishop of Worcester, was able to keep his position for a while, but later lost it as an idiot "who did not know French."[10] Soon, all around England, the Normans used forced English labor to build hundreds of stone castles, including Windsor Castle and the Tower of London, to protect themselves from their new English subjects for, as they complained, "neither fear nor favour could so subdue the English as to prefer peace and tranquility to rebellion and disorders."[11]

A quick sidenote.... Let me note that a number of these castles, such as the Tower of London and Windsor Castle, along with Westminster Abbey and Canterbury Cathedral, incorporated the creamy, easily carved Caen stone which William ordered to be brought to England from Normandy, in hundreds and hundreds of ships. Today they serve as exquisite reminders of both the pain and the beauty that resulted from the Norman Conquest.

15. The Tower of London/16. Windsor Castle/17. Westminster Abbey

And so, within a matter of months, England changed from a country where only a few people spoke French into a country in which the entire upper class conducted its business, legal, educational, artistic, and personal matters in French. Meanwhile, a few bilingual people in the middle worked for the Normans, acted as agents for the Normans in their dealings with the local population, or sold goods to the Normans, goods which were produced by Anglo-Saxon farmers and tradesmen.

Now, let me go back, just a bit, to the day on which William was crowned king. On that day, William still hoped that the English nobles, that is, those who had survived the Battle of Hastings, would submit to him as king. To indicate that he was the true heir of Edward the Confessor and that he did not intend to rock the (official) boat too much, William was crowned king both in French and in English. At first, he also continued the custom of writing government documents in English. However, when the surviving English nobles refused to accept him and began a series of rebellions (1067-1071 and 1075-1076), William moved ruthlessly to eliminate all opposition, laying waste to vast areas of England. He also reversed his position on the official use

PART THREE

of English. From then on, all official documents would be written in Latin.

18. Coronation of William I

"Wait! Wait! Where is Latin going to fit into this story?" you might ask. My focus is on the influence of French on English, but let's take a little detour to discuss Latin. When William of Normandy decided to invade England, a second way for him to persuade French nobles and their armies to support him, in addition to his promise to give them land and positions in England, was to get the approval of the Catholic pope. This would transform William's personal cause into a holy war, (promising forgiveness of sins and eternal life in heaven to his supporters and excommunication from the Catholic church to Harold's supporters). Now, the pope was not happy with the English church for several reasons, including that fact that it wrote its documents in English, not in Latin. Which meant that the pope and church officials in Rome could not understand, much less control, what happened within the English church. After William promised to end this practice, he got the Pope's blessing. And so, after he became king, Latin replaced English as the language of he English church, as well as (as I just mentioned) the language of record for the government.

A few years later, when William's sons came to the throne, the ways in which Latin and French were used began to change and overlap. For example, under William's son, Henry I, Latin continued to be the primary language of official documents in England, but, by 1200, French was also used in government documents. Soon, government officials would sometimes write one document in Latin and another document in French on the very same day! [12] In any case, *for the purposes of this discussion*, I'm going to summarize the topic of the Latin language in this way: Latin was primarily a written language in England and was never spoken by more than a tiny percentage of the population. Therefore, relatively few Latin words entered into English in the first centuries after the Norman Conquest.

The biggest movement of Latin words into English would take place much later, between 1550 and 1660 when the English Renaissance encouraged an explosion of scientific and artistic achievements.[13] Since educated people would already be writing about academic and scientific ideas in Latin, it would be natural that, when they began to write about these ideas in English and couldn't think of an appropriate English word, they would simply insert a familiar Latin word.[14] So, the story of the influence of Latin on English is fascinating, but less dramatic and less complicated than the story of the French influence on English.

Back to 1067, the year after the Conquest. Writing in Old English almost ceased in England. Soon, virtually everything was written either in Latin (which was understood by educated people all over Europe) or in French. With the disappearance of the Anglo-Saxon upper class, Old English was reduced to the status of the spoken language of uneducated peasants. In addition, as lesser landowners and farmers lost their lands to the Normans and became tenants or serfs on the lands that they had once owned, they became tied to the land and no

19. Norman fashions

longer able to travel freely. With so few respected models of correct Old English and the increasing isolation of the various linguistic groups, the (until then very similar) Anglo-Saxon and Norse dialects began to diverge. This would have major implications when English made a comeback a few centuries later. The question then would be: *whose* grammar, *whose* spelling, and *whose* pronunciation would be the new standard English?

Meanwhile, King William filled his court and the top positions in his government with his trusted Norman supporters. How big was this new Norman upper class? Estimates vary. The French-Canadian historian Serge Lusignan suggests that

10,000 Normans and other French arrived in England around 1066.[15] The British historian David Howarth estimates that about 200,000 Normans and other French arrived in England in the twenty years between 1066 and 1086. Both give the population of England in 1066 as about one and a half million people, with Howarth adding that approximately one fifth of the population, or about 300,000 English, died as a result of the death and destruction caused by William's armies.[16]

So, let's go with Lusignan's estimate. Now think about your own country, which certainly has more than one and a half million people. Imagine that all those in positions of power are killed or escape abroad and are replaced by 10,000 people who come from a very different country. And this includes a new king and his supporters who do not speak your language, who know very little about your country, and who conduct all the national affairs in their own language. In fact, these people don't like your country much; they don't like the *weather* or the *language* or the *fashions,* and they really, *really* don't like the *food!* (Perhaps the one thing that the new rulers *do* like is the forests which, once the local population is forbidden to hunt there, offer them excellent game hunting.)

20. Depopulation of Hampshire to form the New Forest

PART THREE

Many of these newcomers have extensive lands in their home country and go back to their country for months or years at a time. In short, many of the people who now rule over you do not understand you and have as little to do with you and your country as possible. Your life will never be the same again and your language may never be the same, either. This is what happened to the English people in 1066.

In **Part Four**, let's see how the English language struggled to survive in a society where French was on the top and English was definitely… on the bottom.

ENTANGLED TONGUES

# PART FOUR

## THE BEGINNING OF THE END OF OLD ENGLISH: THE YEARS AFTER 1066

ENTANGLED TONGUES

PART FOUR

So, here we are in England in 1067, the year after the Conquest. William, Duke of Normandy, has upgraded his name from William the Bastard (because of his parents' relationship) to King William I of England. The English upper class is being replaced by William's trusted Norman supporters. Let's listen to how William Harrison, a 16<sup>th</sup> century English historian, described England at this time:

*After the Saxon tongue, came the... French language over into our country and therein were our laws written for a long time. Our children also were, by an especial decree, taught first to speak the same, and thereunto enforced to learn their constructions in the French, whensoever they were set to the grammar schools. In like sort, few bishops or other clergy men were admitted to any function here among us, but such as came out of religious houses from beyond the seas, to the end that they should not use the English tongue in their sermons to the people. In the court, also, it grew into such contempt that most men thought it no small dishonor to speak any English there. At the last, in the country, every plowman, even the very carters, began to wax weary of their mother tongue and labored to speak French, which then was counted no small token of gentility. And no marvel, for every French rascal, when he came once hither, was taken for a gentleman, only because he was proud and could use his own language. And all this, I say, to exile the English and British speeches quite out of the country.*[17]

Many of the soldiers, priests, monks, merchants, tradespeople, and artisans who came to England immediately after the Conquest came from Normandy. However, increasingly, people arrived from other parts of France, especially the central France/Parisian area, either to take advantage of the opportunities in England or as relatives and servants of the French wives that the English kings continued to seek in France over the next few centuries. (Because of this, from now on, I'm going to call this upper class "Anglo-French" instead of "Anglo-Norman.") These Anglo-French considered Paris to be the center of European culture; many of them traveled back to France as often as they could. William the Conqueror and all other English kings until the late 1400s (except one) married French wives. William was also one of five English kings who were born in France and one of seven English kings who died in France.

Here I'd like to explore a topic which is often neglected, that is, the many ways in which the English and French aristocratic families were interconnected for centuries after the Norman Conquest (thus creating endless opportunities for battles over inheritances). William the Conqueror, while king of England, spent much of his time in France. His son William Rufus (William II) also did. Then the younger brother of William Rufus, Henry I, did the same, protecting his French lands from his nephew William Clito. When Henry I died, his daughter Matilda and her French husband, Geoffrey Plantagenet, were in their Anjou dukedom in France and Henry's nephew Stephen was in Boulogne, in northern France. Stephen made it back to England before Matilda and Geoffrey did, and so he managed to be crowned king. However, he was succeeded by the son of Matilda and Geoffrey who became King Henry II in 1154.

21. The Aquitaine wine trade was very lucrative.

PART FOUR

Henry was already married to Eleanor of Aquitaine (a prosperous region in southwestern France). Combining Aquitaine with his other French territories, Henry II then controlled more French territory than the King of France and had perhaps more French subjects than English subjects![18] Two hundred years later, because of the still close family ties between the French and English royal families, the struggle over who would inherit Aquitaine and its lucrative wine trade would be a factor in the outbreak of the Hundred Years War.

Back to Henry II and Eleanor of Aquitaine. The couple had four sons, of whom the most famous was Richard the Lionheart ("Good King Richard" in the many retellings of the Robin Hood stories). Have you seen any of the movies about (the probably fictional) Robin Hood, the outlaw who lived in Sherwood Forest and stole from the Norman rich to give to the Anglo-Saxon poor?

22. Richard the Lionheart    23. Robin Hood

Do you remember the scene in which King Richard comes into the forest in disguise, speaks to Robin Hood, and suddenly throws back his head covering, so that Robin can see his face? Robin falls to his knees to bow before his king. But... "Richard the Lionheart" was simply a translation of the French name, Richard, Coeur de Lion. And, since this king of England could not speak English, Robin Hood would have had to speak to him in French. In any case, since Richard, Coeur de Lion spent only a few months of his reign in England (for which he "cared not an egg"),[19] Robin Hood would have been lucky to run into him in Sherwood Forest or anywhere else.*

The Anglo-French upper class not only went back and forth between their lands in England and France but also sent their children to be educated in France to ensure that each new generation would keep its French language, culture, and identity. Thus, for many years, the Anglo-French and their new English subjects lived very different lives; their competing vocabularies reflected their two different realities. The Anglo-French lived in *une maison* (which became the English word *mansion*), but most of the population lived in *ein hus*. In the English *hus*, there was a *cook*, but in the French *maison*, there was a *chef*. The English cook might *burn* the meat, but the Anglo-French chef *broiled* it. The peasants raised *cows, sheep, chickens,* and *pigs* which the French ate as *boeuf* (which became *beef), mouton* (which became *mutton), poulet* (which became *poultry),* and *porc* (which became *pork).*

24. Anglo-French life

PART FOUR

In short, for the Anglo-French, life was *aisé*, that is, *easy*, while, for the Anglo-Saxons, life was *hard!*

25. Anglo-Saxon life

Other French words also entered English at this time, words that the Anglo-French were able to impose on their Anglo-Saxon subjects. If you were a servant, you learned the French words: *to boil, to dine, to roast, to serve, table.* If you were accused of a crime, you learned more French words: *jury, trouble, crime, prison, innocent, silence, to prove.* If your landlord were French, you learned *rent* and *paie* (pay), and so on.

It's estimated that about 900 French words came into English in the first century or so after the Conquest.[20] However, another development also affected the fate of the English vocabulary at this time. Remember all the members of the Old English upper class who had fought the Normans and who had been killed or had fled the country? When they disappeared, the vocabulary of Old English literature, music, art, government, law, and so on... went with them.

Now, think for a moment about yourself. I'm sure that you have a much larger *passive* vocabulary in English (the words that you understand) compared to your *active* vocabulary (the words that you actually use). We all do. So did the English people in 1066. Surely, many ordinary people understood the Old English vocabulary of the Anglo-Saxon upper class, without using those words in their own conversations. This meant that they would not pass those words on to their children and grandchildren. And so, within two hundred years after the Conquest, we see that *almost half* of the Old English vocabulary disappeared. (In subsequent centuries, more words disappeared, until about 85% of the Old English vocabulary was lost.)[21] Those Old English words that did survive the first few hundred years after the Conquest tended to be the shorter, basic words that were spoken almost every day by the lower classes. So much so that, today, once you have an English vocabulary of about 6000 words, more of the words that you speak come from French than from Germanic languages, but you still use and repeat the Germanic words (*be, have, see, speak, hear, day, night, born, die,* etc.) much more often...

It's important to underline the fact that, as we said in **Part Two**, Old English produced an impressive body of literature and had a highly sophisticated vocabulary before the Norman Conquest. When we acknowledge this, we can appreciate the fact that, a few centuries later, when English began to absorb an increasing number of French words related to literature, music, art, economics, law, government, and so on, it did not absorb these words because English was inherently a less sophisticated language than French. No. English absorbed those words because *it had to*. As the English language began to reassert itself as a written language in the 14th century, it needed to replace the vocabulary that it had lost after the Norman Conquest. French was the language at hand, so to speak, and therefore it was from French that English found the replacement words that it needed.

PART FOUR

During the years after the Conquest, not only did much of the Old English vocabulary disappear, much of its complicated grammar also disappeared. How did this happen? Well, some of the Old English inflections were already beginning to disappear even before 1066, in part because this made it easier for the Anglo-Saxons and their new Viking neighbors to understand each other. Then, after the Norman Conquest, the lower classes continued to drop inflections which they considered to be unnecessary, unnoticed by academics who were focused on teaching correct Latin and French.

The few examples of Old English writing which have come down to us from the first centuries after the Conquest indicate that Old English retained most synthetic structures for about a hundred years after the Conquest; from then on, there was a sharp reduction in the use of inflections. In the end, Old English lost two of its three different ways of saying *the* (which the German language has kept: *der, die, das*) and ended up with only one word, *the*. It also lost the inflections which showed whether a word was the subject of a verb or the object of a verb. In addition, English lost the verb inflections which indicated whether a person was speaking about the first, second, or third person singular *or* the first, second, or third person plural. Except for one! Can you guess which one? I go, we go, you go, they go, but he or she…? I have, we have, you have, they have, but he or she…? We'll learn more about this souvenir from the past, the third person *-s* ending (as in *goes* and *has*), in **Part Eleven**.

To summarize, within the first two hundred years after the Norman Conquest, English lost almost half of its vocabulary and simplified much of its grammar. By the time the Anglo-French upper class began to speak English, the English that they learned was no longer the complex, nuanced Old English which had been spoken in 1066. That language was gone; that ship had sailed…

Looking back at the impact of the Norman Conquest on his country, the chronicler Robert of Gloucester wrote in 1300:

*Thus came, lo! England into Normandy's hand.*

*And the Normans didn't know how to speak then but their own speech*

*And spoke French as they did at home and their children did also teach.*

*So that high men of this land that of their blood come,*

*Hold all that same speech that they took from them.*

*For, but a man know French, men count of him little…*

*But low men hold to English and to their own speech yet.*

*I think there are in all the world no countries*

*That don't hold to their own speech, but England alone…*[22]

On that sad note, let's end **Part Four** and move on to **Part Five**, where we'll see that the English language did not disappear as Robert of Gloucester feared. As he had good reason to fear! At the time that he wrote, various events had already begun to prepare the ground for the return of English as the one language of England.

---

\* Do you think that Hollywood will ever make a historically accurate movie in which Robin Hood, Richard the Lionheart, the bad King John, and the English barons speak only French? With English subtitles?

# PART FIVE

## MIDDLE ENGLISH: THE HUNDRED YEARS WAR AND THE BLACK DEATH

ENTANGLED TONGUES

PART FIVE

In "The History of English and Its Practical Uses," Fred C. Robinson points out that the Old English sentence "Gecynd mildheortnisse nis oferthrungen" would evolve, within a few hundred years, into Shakespeare's observation in the 1500s that "The quality of mercy is not strained" (i.e. mercy is gentle).²³

How did we get from "Gecynd mildheortnisse nis oferthrungen" to, somewhat later, "The kind of mildheartedness is not overthronged" to Shakespeare's "The quality of mercy is not strained" in only a few hundred years?

Well, *Middle English* is the name that we give to that time period, 1250 to 1500, when English was *transitioning* rapidly from Old English to what we now call Modern English (that is, a merger of Old English and French, with a touch of Latin and a bit of Norse). We can perhaps compare Middle English to the transition from winter to summer which we call spring. In both Middle English and spring, we see constant change, yet the momentum always returns to the same direction. Of course, the change from winter to summer is inevitable, whereas the evolution from Old English to Modern English only seems inevitable in hindsight.

When Robert of Gloucester wrote in 1300, "I think there are in all the world no countries that don't hold to their own speech, but England alone…," he had reason to feel gloomy. Latin was the primary official written language in England, while French was used everywhere in social and professional communication, especially among the upper class. Family issues (requests, quarrels, gossip, etc.) were discussed in conversations held in French and in letters written in French. Regulations, wills, medical prescriptions, building contracts, business contracts, arrangements for travel and lodging, and so on, were written in French. Communications between officials of different towns and even between managers on the large estates (who were typically from the less educated classes) took place in French. Town officials and merchants in England wrote in French to officials and merchants in France and Flanders. Administrators, merchants, and military personnel who were sent to the English-controlled territories in France communicated with the local officials and merchants in French.[24] French was used in England, not only by the upper class, but by virtually any person who exercised a profession.

Now, we need to keep in mind that most of the English people could neither read nor write well in any language; most of the population worked in agriculture or were artisans, manual laborers, servants, etc. However, for the few people who did get an education and who had an opportunity to practice a profession, it was essential to be able to communicate well in French. French was the language of success and English was *not*.

So, where did each new generation learn French? The answer for members of the upper class was "at home, from an early age," with family members and private tutors. Another answer, for the middle class, was "in a song school," run by the Catholic clergy. In such schools, priests taught French to young children until they were old enough to enter a grammar school (thus, teaching the children at an early age when they could internalize a new language quickly and naturally). From there, the children would go to a grammar school where teaching, as well as other activities, would take place in French.[25] Given the number of grammar schools in England, these schools may have produced hundreds of thousands of competent French speakers by the 1300s.[26]*

On the other hand, while the children of many Old English speakers were becoming bilingual to improve their professional and social prospects, some members of the Anglo-French upper class (especially in the lower echelons of the upper class) were marrying outside of their Anglo-French circle, that is, with English speakers (who were, almost certainly, bilingual). And, beginning in the 1200s, a series of events must have suggested to the Anglo-French nobility that perhaps they were not *so* French,

## PART FIVE

as they began to distinguish themselves from the newcomers who continued to arrive from France. They were especially upset about the French relatives and advisors that King Henry III allowed to live at his court, where they gave him bad advice and spent lots of money, while showing disdain for the heavily taxed Anglo-French nobles who were footing the bill for all of this.

26. Henry III and his barons

As Roger of Wendover, in his *Flowers of History*, described the court of Henry III in 1233:

*The king also invited men from Poitou and Brittany who were poor and covetous after wealth and two thousand knights and soldiers... used their utmost endeavors to oppress the natural English subjects and nobles...and wherever the king went he was surrounded by crowds of these foreigners, and nothing was done in England except what the bishop of Winchester and his host of foreigners determined on.*[27]

Now, why would Henry III invite so many Frenchmen to live off of him at his court? Well, one reason was that his mother, Isabella, was French (of course) and, after the death of her husband, King John, she went back to France, married a French noble, and had nine more children. Many of these children and other relatives ended up in Henry III's English court.** Later, Henry acquired more French relatives when he married Eleanor of Provence (whose older sister Margaret was married to the king of France, Louis IX).

Louis. That name rings a bell. So, let's go back, just a bit, to Henry III's father, the *bad* King John, who in the Robin Hood stories, became king after his brother, the *good* King Richard (Richard Coeur de Lion), died. Well, this King John, who refused to abide by the Magna Carta, was hated by much of the nobility. So much so that a contingent of barons went to Prince Louis of France and offered to support him if he would invade England and dethrone King John. Prince Louis *did* invade England and ended up controlling about two-thirds of the kingdom.[28] He was acknowledged as the true king by many English nobles and by the king of Scotland, and was well on his way to being crowned, when King John suddenly died. Immediately, King John's supporters had John's nine-year-old son crowned King Henry III. At this point, some of Prince Louis' supporters began to rethink their opposition to the new young king who promised that, in contrast to this father, he would abide by the Magna Carta.*** One by one, Prince Louis' supporters defected to the young Henry. Finally, Prince Louis returned to France where he became King Louis VIII at his father's death.

This is only one example of the bullets that the English language dodged in the centuries after the Norman Conquest. If King John hadn't eaten so much questionable fish or fruit one day and gotten food poisoning (if, in fact, that's why he died), he and his supporters may well have been beaten by the French

PART FIVE

prince who would surely have sent King John into exile, or worse. England would have been united with France into one kingdom under a King Louis and his descendants, perhaps for a long time...

Now, this French Prince Louis had a son, also named Louis, who became King Louis IX of France. Louis IX later became the brother-in-law of Henry III, the son of King John whom his father had sought to dethrone.

In 1244, Louis IX issued a decree which stated, "As it is impossible that any man living in my kingdom and having possessions in England can competently serve two masters, he must either inseparably attach himself to me or to the king of England." [29] When Henry III heard this, not to be outdone by his brother-in-law (with whom, in spite of everything, he had a good relationship, spending Christmas together and all that), he issued a similar statement. It seems that such decrees were not strictly enforced, but their existence did encourage the Anglo-French in England to split up their lands and to give their lands in England to one child and their lands in France to another child. Thus, the children who inherited land only in France were almost sure to *leave England* while the children who inherited land only in England had little choice but to *stay in England*. From then on, their future and their children's future would be an English future, and this English future would increasingly include the English language.

In the next century, we'll see another reason for those Anglo-French who stayed in England to learn English. Which brings us to the Hundred Year's War...

In 1327, King Edward III, the son of Edward II and Isabella of France (another Isabella), came to the throne. Edward's mother was the sister of the French king, Charles IV. (It was largely due to her influence that Parisian French replaced Norman French as

~ 51 ~

ENTANGLED TONGUES

27. Reinforcements during the Hundred Years Was/The fleur-de-lys was on the English royal coat of arms until 1801.

the language of the English court in the 1300s.) After the death of Charles IV in 1328, Edward III believed that he, as his nephew, should become the next king of France. He then added the fleur-de-lys, the symbol of French royalty, to his own coat of arms and began to assert his claim to the French throne.

And so, France and England began a war which lasted, with fighting off and on, for more than a century: the Hundred Years War (1337-1453). In England, French became the language of the enemy. And, as a practical matter, at the Battle of Crécy in 1346, many Anglo-French nobles had such difficulty communicating with their own foot soldiers that, after the battle, Edward III's son, the Black Prince, ordered them to learn English.

However, during this on-again, off-again war, personal and family ties continued to be strong. For example, in 1356, the Black

PART FIVE

Prince captured King John II of France and brought him as a "prisoner" to England, where he received a warm reception from King Edward III, Queen Philippa, and the Queen Mother, Isabella (who was "the prisoner's" first cousin). King John lived in luxury in England and often visited the king, the queen, and the queen mother, who exchanged books, ideas, and music with him.

28. The Black Prince presents the prisoner King John to his father

Of course, all of this visiting and exchanging of books and all of these chats about the latest in French fashion and art took place in French. Eventually, King John negotiated a ransom and returned to France, but when he was not able to come up with the total amount of his ransom, he appointed his son as his regent and voluntarily returned to England, where King Edward and Queen Philippa welcomed him again. According to witnesses, "Between then and supper, there was time for much dancing and merriment. It would be impossible to record all the honours with which the King and Queen received King John." [30] And when they all went to London for more entertainment, feasts, music, and tournaments, they were met by cheering crowds of Londoners.

In sum, the Hundred Years War was a war like no other. The fighting was off-and-on and the actual battles were few.**** In between the fighting and even during the fighting, family and cultural ties continued to assert themselves. Yes, these ties were weakening, but they still remained.

As if the Hundred Years War were not enough for the English people to deal with, in June 1348, the Black Death arrived in England, most likely coming on ships bringing wine from the city of Bordeaux in Aquitaine. Within a few years, 30% or more of the population died. The Catholic clergy died in especially high numbers, since priests and nuns who went out to help the sick and dying brought the Black Death back to their monasteries and convents, where it killed other priests, nuns, and monks.

29. The Black Death

PART FIVE

This was not only a human disaster but also a disaster for the status of the French language in England. As I mentioned earlier, the Catholic clergy were in charge of most schools in England, including the "song schools" in which young children learned French to prepare them for the grammar schools where everything would take place in French. After the Black Death, less educated people who spoke little or no French had to be recruited from the countryside to replace the many teachers who had died. And so, by 1385, the use of French as the language of instruction in schools had become rare and the use of English as the language of instruction had become common.*****

As John of Trevisa, a fellow at Queen's College, Oxford, complained in 1385:

*now, the year of our lord one thousand three hundred four score and five... children of grammar school know no more French than their left heel.... and that is harmful for them...*[31]

In sum, during the 1200s and 1300s, intermarriage, a resentment of French newcomers at the English court, the custom of giving English lands to one child and French lands to another child, the need for the nobility to communicate with the soldiers that they commanded, and, above all, the loss of so many French-speaking teachers due to the Black Death, combined to shift the momentum *away from* an increasing use of French in England and *toward* an increasing use of English.

In 1362, Parliament opened for the first time in English and, that same year, issued a statute (written in French!) which required court cases to be conducted in English[32] However, this order may have been issued more as a way to increase patriotism and, thus, support for the Hundred Years War than as a way to increase the use of English.[33] In any case, this statute was widely ignored. And, of course, we need to remember that the English of 1362 was no longer the English of Harold Godwinson. By the late

1300s, it was impossible to write an official English text without using French loanwords or to practice law without using the French words which, by then, had defined English law for three centuries.³⁴

In **Part Six**, we'll continue to discuss how English slowly replaced French throughout England.

---

\* David Trotter (2003) questions the conclusion (based on comparisons of *literary* texts written in France to *non-literary* texts written in England) that the French spoken in England was inferior to the French spoken in France.³⁵ Suggett (1946) points out that early French language manuals which appeared in England were not used to teach the French language itself, as so many people seem to believe. Instead, these manuals assumed prior French fluency and sought to teach eloquence and the proper way to address people of various social statuses.³⁶

\*\* Henry III's son Edward I was the first king since Harold Godwinson to be given an Anglo-Saxon name. William the Conqueror had a French name, of course, and was followed by his sons: Henry, Stephen, Richard, John, and Robert. Before and after the Conquest, Emma (of Normandy), Eleanor (of Aquitaine), Catherine (de Valois), and Margaret (of Anjou) became English queens and brought their French names with them to England. All of these names which now seem so English were French imports.

\*\*\* In *Louis: The French Prince Who Invaded England*, Catherine Hanley (2016) concludes, "Had Louis not invaded, it is likely that the baronial rebellion would have been crushed; Magna Carta might well have been annulled and forgotten, relegated to a footnote in history as the monarchy forged ahead unabated and unanswerable to the law. Louis's part in tempering royal authority therefore left a legacy to the English which is still being felt to this day." ³⁷

PART FIVE

\*\*\*\* During the Hundred Years War, which was fought primarily on French soil, battles were, in fact, rare. More common than battles (which led to the deaths of experienced and, therefore, valuable English soliders) were the sieges and chevauchées (that is, quick raids in which the English looted, burned houses and crops, and killed or stole the livestock that made farming possible) which led to the deaths of many peasants and townspeople throughout France.

\*\*\*\*\* Analyses of French language texts written in England during the late 1300s show a dramatic increase in the type of errors that are typically made by someone who has learned a language at school, rather than by acquiring it naturally in early childhood, as was done in the English "song schools." In the view of Richard Ingham (2014), the timing of the Black Death and the subsequent collapse in French fluency "is too close to be a coincidence." [38]

ENTANGLED TONGUES

# PART SIX

## THE MIDDLE ENGLISH PERIOD: RICHARD II, HENRY IV, AND HENRY V/THE END OF THE HUNDRED YEARS WAR

ENTANGLED TONGUES

PART SIX

30. Young Richard II speaks to the rebels in English

In 1377, Richard II (1367-1400) became king on the death of his grandfather, King Edward III, who had entertained King John of France so lavishly. (Richard's father was the Black Prince who, before his early death, had captured King John and had ordered the Anglo-French nobles to learn English.) Richard was born in Aquitaine, his father's principality in France at that time, and taken care of by French nannies, making French his likely first language. However, it seems that he did speak English (although we don't know how well); his speech to the peasants during the Peasants' Revolt in 1381 was the first recorded use of English by an English king since Harold Godwinson.[39] Unlike his father and many of the English nobles, Richard II did not love the idea of fighting France; after his beloved wife Anne died, he arranged a marriage with Isabella, the young daughter of the French king, Charles VI, in an effort to achieve peace.

# ENTANGLED TONGUES

Richard II's court was famous for its luxury and its poetry. One poet there, John Gower, wrote a treatise on marriage "en français, à tout le monde" ("in French, to everyone"),[40] implying that French was the language in which writers could reach the most people. However, we also see in this court a new generation of writers and poets who not only wrote in French and translated literary works from French but also wrote in English.

The most famous of these was Geoffrey Chaucer, the author of *The Canterbury Tales*. Chaucer (whose name comes from the French *Chaussier)* absorbed the French language and culture from an early age; he grew up in the aristocratic household of Elizabeth de Burgh and her husband, Prince Lionel (who was the son of Edward III, the brother of the Black Prince, *and the uncle of Richard II)*. Therefore, Chaucer would have spoken the Parisian French which had replaced the now less fashionable Norman French at the English court. This may help us to understand his gentle mockery, in his *Canterbury Tales*, of Madame Eglantine who, Chaucer tells us, spoke French "after the school of Stratford-at-Bowe, for French of Paris was to her unknown."

Chaucer married the daughter of a French knight, spent time on the European continent on military and diplomatic missions for the king (which would have been conducted in French) and translated French literary works into English, notably *Le Roman de la Rose*, one of the most popular poems of the later Middle Ages. The French historian, Édouard Le Héricher, calls Chaucer "presque un Français" ("practically a Frenchman").[41] And, as Ardis Butterfield writes in "Chaucer's French Inheritance," "By allowing ourselves to see French as a natural language for Chaucer… we can better appreciate the truly international character of his English."[42]

Different writers give different estimates of the percentage of Chaucer's vocabulary which comes from French, but one estimate

PART SIX

31. *The Canterbury Tales* (detail of the North Reading Room mural)

is as high as 51%.[43] Now, Chaucer is, of course, celebrated as "the father of English literature" and his *Canterbury Tales* is said to signal the rebirth of that literature. However, with its analytic sentence structures and its many words of French origin (for example, *difficult* and *edifice* as synonyms for *hard* and *building* as well as *experience* and *authority* as replacements for Old English words which had been lost), *The Canterbury Tales* would hardly have been understood by Harold Godwinson and his court. So, is it accurate to say that *The Canterbury Tales* signaled a *rebirth*? Or did it signal *the emergence of a new hybrid language*, a "Frenglish," or Middle English, which was on its way to becoming our Modern English?

While various members of Richard's court were writing in English as well as in French, other writers were translating religious commentary and even the Bible into English. The most famous of these was John Wycliffe of Oxford University who insisted that an English version of the Bible should be made available to all English Christians. Now this idea was anathema to people such as Thomas Arundel, the Archbishop of Canterbury and Chancellor of England, who saw the spread of religious ideas in English as a threat to his religious and political power. Arundel ended up taking part in a rebellion against Richard II and was exiled to France where he teamed up with Richard's cousin and childhood playmate, Henry Bolingbroke, who was also in exile. *

Without permission from the king, Bolingbroke and Arundel returned to England in 1399. At first, Bolingbroke pledged his loyalty to Richard but later tricked him into leaving his castle, captured him, and forced him to abdicate. Then Bolingbroke had Richard murdered, most likely by starvation. One eyewitness to all this was Jean Creton, who had been sent to the English court by the French king (Richard's father-in-law) and was with Richard at this time. According to Creton, he was with the two cousins and

32. Meeting of Richard and Henry

heard every word of their final very emotional conversations, in which Henry insisted that his motive for returning was "to help" Richard to govern. Creton's testimony indicates that the cousins must have been speaking to each other in French.[44]**

And so, Henry Bolingbroke was crowned King Henry IV in October 1399, and Thomas Arundel resumed his old position as Archbishop of Canterbury. With their new powers, Henry IV and Arundel made the translation of religious materials into English punishable by burning at the stake (*De Heretico Comburendo*). Henry also persecuted those nobles who did not switch their loyalties to

PART SIX

him quickly enough. Sir John Montagu, the poet, was killed about the same time that King Richard was murdered and, a few months later, Geoffrey Chaucer simply disappeared. We don't know for sure when, where, or how Chaucer died, or what happened to his manuscripts. Strangely, there was no notice of the funeral or burial of the man who, according to the poet, John Lydgate, ...

> *First began to enlarge our language*
>
> *And adorn it with his eloquence*
>
> *To whom honour and praise and reverence*
>
> *Throughout this land be given and sung* [45]

Chaucer had been popular and honored at Richard's court, had praised Richard as "lord of this language," [46] and, in *The Canterbury Tales*, had ruthlessly mocked the churchmen who used church revenues, taken from the poor, to live in luxury, as did Archbishop Arundel. In addition, in *The Canterbury Tales*, Chaucer presented the Clerk of Oxford in a positive light. (Oxford, you'll remember, was the home of Arundel's nemesis, John Wycliffe.) Perhaps worst of all, from the archbishop's point of view, Chaucer's parson, in "The Parson's Tale," quoted from the Bible in English! Was Chaucer murdered? This question is raised, but left unanswered in the book *Who Murdered Chaucer?* (Jones, 2003).

Back to the new king, Henry IV. Whatever Henry IV's position was on allowing the translation of religious materials into English, he was quite ready to use the appeal of the English language for his own ends. Having dethroned Richard II, the lawful ruler, Henry was obsessed with establishing his legitimacy as king and so, when he was crowned, he made a speech in English, his "mother tongue." [47]*** However, Henry IV never again spoke or wrote in English for official purposes.[48]

An interesting note from Henry's reign has survived. In 1403, the Dean of Windsor, in the middle of a battle, wrote to the new king. He began his letter in French, as usual, then switched into English, and hurriedly finished with *"Escript a Hereford, en tres graunte haste, a trois de la clocke apres noone, le tierce jour de Septembre."* [49] Obviously, the Dean felt obliged to begin his letter in French, but had to switch to English, being unable to write French quickly enough. And yet, he still felt that he needed to end his letter in (some form of) French.

As it turns out, Henry IV had a son, also named Henry, who had grown up in Richard II's court and who, according to one chronicler, "loved him (Richard II) entirely." At first, the boy refused to obey his father's command to leave Richard II after he was captured. At one point, however, Richard spoke to the boy, telling him that he needed to obey his father, adding, "I know well there is one Henry shall do me much harm; and I suppose it is not thou. Wherefore I pray thee be my friend, for I... (know) ... not how it will go." Ultimately, the boy left Richard, "with a heavy heart," to join his father.[50]**** It was this Prince Henry who, even before his father's death, began to revive the memory of Richard's court in which writers such as Chaucer had flourished.

In 1412, Prince Henry commissioned a book about Troy from the poet John Lydgate. According to Lydgate, he did this:

*Because he wished that to high and low*

*The noble story might be openly known*

*In our tongue, everywhere in every age,*

*And written as well in our language*

*As it is in Latin and French* [51]

PART SIX

The next year, when young Henry came to the throne as Henry V, one of his first acts would be to return Richard II's body from his father's private estate to Westminster Abbey in London, where he had it buried with much ceremony.

Although Henry V was probably the first king to speak and write English with ease, he initially continued to use French in his personal letters and official pronouncements. Then, in August 1417, for reasons which are still not clear, he abruptly switched to English in letters to his subjects and to government officials. These letters, many of which were written about upcoming government actions, were copied by the clerks in the Chancery, where government documents were printed and then sent all over England. Thus, the writing style of Henry V, that is, "the King's English," served as a model of English usage, increasing the consistency of spelling and grammar throughout England.

During the reign of Henry V, the French language lost most of its administrative functions in England. In addition, many private organizations, such as the Brewers Guild, switched over to English at this time, citing the king's use of English and the model of the Chancery Standard, as well as their own members' difficulties with French. However, there were exceptions to this observation. First, the increasingly out-of-touch "Law French" (incomprehensible to English speakers and French speakers alike!) continued to be used by lawyers as late as the early 1600s, to maintain their professional monopoly.***** Doctors, too, were eager to retain a monopoly on medical information; as one man warned, "there were too many books set forth in the English tongue... and... the Art (of medicine) is thereby made common... for that, every gentleman is as well able to reason therein as ourselves." [52] And the English nobility, well able to afford private tutors for their children, continued for centuries to value the ability to speak and write excellent French as a sign of their high status.

~ 67 ~

33. Henry V at the Battle of Agincourt

Henry V turned out to be a warrior king who was determined to unite France and England under one king, that is, himself. He believed, as did all English kings since Edward III, that he was the lawful king of France. After his amazing victory at the Battle of Agincourt, Henry forced Charles VI of France to give him his daughter, Catherine, as his wife and to name him as his heir, thus

34. Henry V weds Catherine, daughter of Charles VI and sister of Richard II's second wife, Isabella

disinheriting the French king's own son. However, Henry V died two months before Charles VI died, so we'll never know what would have happened to the English language if Henry V had achieved his goal of becoming king of both England and France.

Henry's son, Henry VI (1421-1471), became king of England at his father's early death, and, a few weeks later, king of France at the death of his grandfather, Charles VI, all before the age of one year. But the young Henry VI grew up to be a gentle and pious young man, not a king who could inspire an army of soldiers, as his father had done. And as a young woman, Joan of Arc, was able to do in France for Charles VII, the son of Charles VI (and thus Henry VI's maternal uncle), who, unsurprisingly, claimed the French throne for himself. After Joan of Arc arrived in the French city of Orléans in 1429, she wrote to the English army in French, suggesting an exchange of prisoners. Immediately, the English officers replied in French, calling her "vachère" and "putain des Armagnacs," which I will leave untranslated.[53] So, we see that, in 1429, many English army officers were still very capable of expressing their feelings vividly and spontaneously in French.

35. Joan of Arc

In her book *Honi Soit Qui Mal Y Pense*, the French linguist Henriette Walter writes, "L'histoire conjointe du français et de l'anglais semble en tout cas s'arrêter net après Jeanne d'Arc." [54] ("The common history of French and English seems, in any case, to come to a dead stop after Joan of Arc.") In Walter's view, without the intervention of Joan of Arc, England might well have won the Hundred Years War. In which case, the union of England and France into one kingdom under Henry VI (the French-speaking son of a French princess, married to a French noblewoman) would likely have led to a very different linguistic outcome in England.

To summarize our discussion of the Hundred Years War: when Edward III began this war with dreams of uniting England and France under his rule, the use of French was at its peak in England, King Edward spoke only French, and England controlled vast amounts of land in France, with much of the royal income coming from the wine trade in Aquitaine. However, by the end of this war, the use of English for both personal and professional communication was the norm in England, Henry VI spoke fluent English, and England had lost virtually all of its French territories. In addition, with the loss of opportunities in France for military action, for lucrative trade deals, and for high-paying administrative positions, there were many fewer incentives for the ambitious to prioritize fluency in French.

Yet, hindsight is 20/20. *We* may conclude that the common history of England and France ended with the Hundred Years War, but English kings continued to claim, for many years, that they were the rightful kings of France.

In **Part Seven**, we'll see how these historical events worked to transform the English language.

# PART SIX

\* Henry IV and Richard II shared a French grandmother and both of them spent some of their early years in France.

\*\* Jean Creton was only one of the many French observers who, over the centuries, attempted to send back to France accurate reports of the people and events in England. These reports give us a valuable alternative to the English accounts, produced with an eye to the approval of the occupant of the English throne.

\*\*\* There are two reasons to reserve judgment about this reference to Henry's "mother tongue." First, as a new king of dubious legitimacy, he surely chose his words carefully to appeal to his subjects' emotions. Second, a statement such as "English was his mother tongue" or even the statement" He spoke English" tells us very little unless we know how well he spoke English, say, on a scale of 1-10. To assess Henry's mastery of English, we need to look for additional evidence elsewhere. The fact that Henry spoke French in his his official acts and in private conversations to family members and never wrote in English suggest the his mastery of English was limited.

\*\*\*\* This conversation between Richard II and the young Henry, like all of their conversations, almost certainly took place in French.

\*\*\*\*\* It was not until 18th century, with the Statute of 1731, that French was finally eliminated from English law.

ENTANGLED TONGUES

# PART SEVEN

## A HUGE INFUSION OF FRENCH WORDS INTO ENGLISH, 1250 TO 1500

ENTANGLED TONGUES

PART SEVEN

As I said earlier, in the two centuries after the Norman Conquest, about 900 words moved from French into English, that is, about 900 French words were *imposed* on the English population by the new French-speaking ruling class. However, from about 1250 to about 1500, as more and more English speakers also spoke French and then as more and more French speakers also spoke English,[55] we see over 10,000 words move from French into English. These words were different in three ways from the imposed words that had entered English in the years after the Conquest. First, these were French words which bilingual speakers (knowing that their companions understood French) might insert into their everyday English conversations when an English word did not express exactly what they wanted to say, when they could not remember the right English word, or when the English word simply didn't feel right.

In addition, as more and more writers were using English, they needed appropriate words to express their thoughts about government, philosophy, art, music, etc., that is, they needed new words to replace the vocabulary that had been lost in the years after the Norman Conquest. As the English historian Charles Barber writes, "...when the bilingual speakers were changing over to English for such purposes as government and literature, they felt the need for the specialized terms that they were accustomed to in those fields and brought them over from French." [56]

Finally, beginning in the 14th century, new words came more often from Parisian/Central French than from Norman French, as the English control of Normandy weakened and as English kings brought French wives from other parts of France.[57]

Here are only a few of the words and expressions that came into English at that time: *action, actual, certain, common, continue, cost, cruel, destroy, dozen, fault, flatter, honest, inform, join, number, opinion, push, real, season, secret, stranger, to learn something by heart, to make believe,* and *for good.* As all of these words and expressions came into English, there was a great deal of duplication. In some cases, the French word eventually disappeared, but more often it was the Old English word that was lost.⁵⁸ For example, the Old English word *earm* (*arm* in modern German) was replaced by the French word *pauvre* and so now we say *poor* instead of *arm*. The Old English *leod* (*leute* in modern German) was replaced by the French *peuple* and now we say *people*. The Old English word *belifan* (*bleiben* in modern German) was replaced by the French-origin verb *to remain*, and so on.

When both the French word and the Old English word stayed in the language, one of them needed to develop new connotations. Why was that? Well, languages do not usually allow for true synonyms: they typically kill off exact synonyms when they appear. So, for both words to survive in English, at least one of them needed to shift its meaning a bit, so that the two words could become alternatives to each other, rather than direct competitors.

Now, there's an exception in English to what I've just said and that is in the law. After 1066, many legal phrases came into use which contained an Old English word as well as its French synonym, thus guaranteeing that the phrase would be understood by both English and French speakers. (Today, the meanings of the two words are somewhat different, but, for some time, they were the same.) In these legal phrases, the Old English word usually comes first and a French synonym comes second. However, in one of the following phrases, the French word comes first. See if you can spot the phrase in which the French word comes first. Here they are: (to own something) *free and clear*, (the crime of) *breaking and entering*, *to indemnify and hold harmless* (against liability and loss), a *true and correct* (copy of a document), a person's *last will and testament*, *to acknowledge and confess*. (Answer: *to indemnify and hold harmless*.)

As I said earlier, languages don't usually allow for words with the exact same meaning. When you look up a word in an English-

PART SEVEN

English dictionary and you see a list of synonyms, those synonyms are simply the words that are *closest* in meaning to the original word. They are not "identical twin" words; they are "sister/brother" words or even "cousin" words, that is, they are *similar, but not the same.* Do you remember, from **Part One**, the Old English word *hus* which became *house* and the French word *maison* which became *mansion* in English? These words began with the same meaning, but, in order for both words to survive in English, the word *mansion* developed its own distinct meaning and became a *big, expensive, impressive* house.

To illustrate this a bit more, let's look at several pairs of synonyms, with the Old English word first and the French-origin word second. (See if you can feel a slight difference in the way that you respond to each of the two synonyms.) *Friendly/amiable, big/grand, deep/profound, to understand/to comprehend, to help/to aid, to weep/to cry, to feed/to nourish, to answer/to respond,* and *to ask/to demand.*

When you compare "She asked for a refund" to "She demanded a refund," you'll notice that *to demand* has acquired an aggressive connotation in English which the French word *demander* doesn't have. By the way, did you notice the only word pair in the last paragraph in which the second word, from French, is used more in daily conversation than the first word, from Old English? Let's look at the list again: *friendly/amiable, big/grand, deep/profound, to understand/to comprehend, to help/to aid, to weep/to cry, to feed/to nourish, to answer/to respond,* and *to ask/to demand.* (Answer: *to weep/to cry.*)

While the meanings of many French words have shifted only slightly since they came into English, a few French-origin words have taken on completely different meanings in English, creating confusion, for example, when someone mixes up the English word *sympathetic* and the French word *sympathique* or the English word *actually* and the French word *actuellement.* In English, a *sympathetic* person is a good companion if you feel very sad. This person will probably send you a *sympathy* card if you have a death in your family. However, if you go out in France on a Friday night, you want a companion who's *sympathique*, that is, very likeable, nice to be with, etc. In English, if I tell you that a snowstorm is *actually* predicted in Saudi Arabia (that is, is truly, in fact predicted), I'm expressing my surprise at this unexpected occurrence, but if I say, in France, that some cheap tickets to the World Cup are available *actuellement*, (that is, right now), you may hurry to buy them before this amazing discount ends. And so on. It's easy to be misunderstood if one trusts too much in the similarity of English and French words.

Now, may I add another complication to all of this? Many discussions of the English language will say that there are three primary sources of English vocabulary: German, French, and Latin. Which is true. However, it's more complicated than that. First, within the category of Germanic languages, we have Old English (Anglo-Saxon) and Norse (Viking) synonyms, such as the Old English word *sick* and the Norse word *ill*, the Old English *hide* and the Norse *skin*, the Old English *craft* and the Norse *skill*, the Old English *to* and the Norse *till*, and so on.

In addition, we have Parisian French and Norman French synonyms, such as the Parisian words *evaluate*, *law*, and *annul* versus *assess*, *bill*, and *cancel*, which come from Norman French. There were also French words that began one way in Parisian French and another way in Norman French, giving us *guarantee*, which begins with the Parisian *g*-sound, versus *warranty*, which begins with the Norman *w*- sound. We have the Parisian *guardian* versus the Norman *warden*, *guerilla* versus *warrior*, and *Guillaume le Conquérant* versus *William the Conqueror*. Finally, we have words which, in Parisian French, began with a *ch*- whereas, in Norman French, the same word began with only a *c*-, such as *channel* versus *canal* and *chattel* versus *cattle*. After they arrived in England, these words developed different meanings to go with their different spellings and pronunciation.

As if all that were not enough to make English "a hodgepodge of all other speeches," there's one more factor to consider. While English was evolving, the French language was evolving, too! So, today English contains many words from Old French, as it was spoken between the 11$^{th}$ and 14$^{th}$ centuries, in addition to other words from Middle French, as it was spoken between the 14$^{th}$ and 17$^{th}$ centuries. Many words which came from Middle French into English still survive in spoken French today. However, many of the words which came from Old French into English have survived in their English form but are no longer used in modern French. One example is the English word *plenty,* as in "There's no rush. We have plenty of time." *Plenté* was an Old French word which meant *abundance.* However, *plenté* fell out of use in French in the 17$^{th}$ century and now exists only in English, as *plenty.*[59] In addition, a past habit could be signaled by the Old French verb *user,* which disappeared from French but continues in English, as in "She used to be shy, but now she enjoys meeting new people." [60]

No wonder that the French linguist Henriette Walter writes that English students find it easier to understand Old French than French students do! [61] Or that the British linguist John Orr writes, "For the Frenchman of today, English… is somewhat of a museum of his own linguistic antiquities." [62]

In **Part Eight,** we'll discuss a few exceptions to my rule that, in English, French always wins.

ENTANGLED TONGUES

# PART EIGHT

## THE POWER OF OLD ENGLISH/ COMET WORDS

ENTANGLED TONGUES

PART EIGHT

I have been giving you an expanded version of the lecture that I used to give on the first day of classes for English language teachers who came from all around the world to study language teaching methodologies at the University of California. This is the moment in my lecture when I would say, "In English, French always wins," that is, words of French origin are more elegant, used more in intellectual and academic discussions, etc. whereas words of Germanic origin are more basic and used more in daily life. And there is truth in that. However, with time, I've modified my statement. Now I would say that, in English, words of French origin often "win" by being perceived as more elegant and intellectual, but that words of Germanic origin sometimes "win" by being more emotionally powerful. Simply compare your own reactions to the Germanic-origin words *wife, funny,* and *forgive* versus *spouse, amusing,* and *pardon* which come from French. As the 19th century American poet, Eugene Field (1850-1895) put it:

*I like the Anglo-Saxon speech*

*With its direct revealings*

*It takes a hold and seems to reach*

*Way down into your feelings* [63]

Now, think about an English speaker who locks himself out of his car in a blizzard or who sees a shark coming towards his small boat. You can bet that the first words that come out of his mouth will not come from French! More likely, they will be a modern (four-letter) version of the very same Germanic words that the English army muttered at the Battle of Hastings when they saw that Harold Godwinson had fallen.

On a happier note, consider the words from the Anglican *Book of Common Prayer* (commissioned by Edward VI in 1549) which we still repeat when we get married: "I take thee to be my wedded husband/wife, to have and to hold from this day forward, for better, for worse, for richer, for poorer, in sickness and in health..." Only two words come from French; can you guess which ones? (Answer: *rich* and *poor*). Or consider this sentence, again from the *Book of Common Prayer*, that we repeat when someone dies, "Earth to earth, ashes to ashes, dust to dust." How many words come from French? (Answer: *none*.)

When Winston Churchill spoke to the English people during World War II, he inspired them by declaring, "We shall fight on the beaches, we shall fight on the landing grounds, we shall fight in the fields and in the streets, we shall fight in the hills; we shall never surrender." Only the final word *surrender* comes from French; every other word is Germanic. On the American side, if we look at Martin Luther King's "I Have a Dream" speech, we can see how he reached into his listeners' hearts, not by using words from French and saying, "Finally at liberty," but by using only Germanic words to say, "Free at last! Free at last! Thank God Almighty, we are free at last!"

Recently, I heard the beautiful song "Angel Standing By" by the American singer Jewel. Which words in the lyrics below do you think come from French?

*All through the night, I'll be watching over you*

*And all through the night, I'll be standing over you*

*And through bad dreams, I'll be right there*

*Telling you everything's gonna be alright*

*And when you cry, I'll be there*

*Telling you, you're never nothing less than beautiful*

*So don't you worry. I'm your angel standing by...*

PART EIGHT

Which words above come from French? (Answer: 1-*cry* and 2- *beautiful*, which combines the French word *beauté* with the Anglo-Saxon suffix -*ful* and therefore is half-French.) The word *angel* came from Latin into Old English, in 597 or so, as you may remember from **Part Two**. Everything else is Germanic.

Jewel instinctively knew that "watching over you" would have more emotional impact than the French-derived "protecting you," just as Martin Luther King sensed that he should say, "I have a dream" and not "I have a rêverie." Churchill knew he would inspire the British public more with "We shall fight ... in the streets, we shall fight in the hills" than with "We shall fight in the avenues, we shall fight in the mountains." Great orators and song writers instinctively know, that "Anglo-Saxon speech" "takes a hold" and reaches "way down into your feelings."

Now, there is a second exception to my initial conclusion that, in English, French always wins. That is the use of Germanic words which I like to describe as "comet words." Remember Halley's Comet? The ball of ice with a long tail that goes around the sun and passes by the earth every 76 years. Comets are beautiful, we must look up to see them, and we rarely see them.

What I call "comet words" are Old English words that managed to survive the Norman Conquest by creating their own little language niches with very specific connotations. Whereas today most Germanic-origin words in English are basic, everyday words, these "comet words" are less common and more literary than their French synonyms. For example, compare "He *rued* his words" to "He *regretted* his words." The Old English verb *to rue* one's words or actions means to regret them, painfully, deeply, and at length. And, while most people probably *rue* at least one unfortunate thing that they have done in their lives, only a very few people will ever use the Old English verb *to rue* instead of its more common French-origin synonym, *to regret*.

Another comet word, which passes by us more often, is the word *fraught*. *To be fraught with something* is to be full of something unpleasant, such as problems or dangers, as in the sentence, "Their plan to escape the island was fraught with difficulty." This connotation of hidden difficulties and dangers is missing in its much more common French-origin synonyms *to involve/to be accompanied by*. And how about the now rarely used Old English verb *to bid someone to do something?* There is a sweet touch of gentleness in *to bid someone to do something*, compared to its French-origin synonyms *to command/to order someone to do something*.

So, we can say that, in English, French *mostly* wins. However, there are these other words, these Old English "comet words" which are so emotionally and esthetically charged that, when we use them, they elevate our speech, our dramas, and our poetry. And, because they are rarely used in daily life, they present a challenge to non-native speakers who study the works of writers such as Shakespeare, who writes so beautifully in *MacBeth*, "Give sorrow words. The grief that does not speak whispers the *o'erfraught* heart and *bids* it break."

In **Part Nine**, we'll discuss four aspects of English which sometimes drive English language learners crazy: phrasal verbs, the present perfect, the present continuous, and irregular verbs.

# PART NINE

### PHRASAL VERBS/THE PRESENT PERFECT/THE PRESENT CONTINOUS/IRREGULAR VERBS

ENTANGLED TONGUES

PART NINE

Up to this point, we've been comparing individual Old English words to their French-origin synonyms. Now let's look at another type of English verb, that is, phrasal verbs (which are sometimes called two-word verbs). Then we'll discuss three aspects of English grammar which also give English language learners headaches (and which we may be able to tie to the Norman Conquest).

Phrasal verbs are verbs which result from the combination of a short Old English verb, such as *to run*, with one or two prepositions, such as *into*, to create a new verb, for example, *to run into someone or something*. The words *run* and *into* lose their original identities as verbs or prepositions and act together to form this new phrasal verb, *to run into*. That is, *the meaning of a phrasal verb is independent of the meaning of the verb and the preposition or prepositions which form it*. For example, when we say, "Robin Hood ran into Richard the Lionheart in Sherwood Forest" or "My friend ran into financial problems after his accident," no one was *running* anywhere. The verb is not *to run*; the verb is *to run into*. The two words act as a single, indivisible unit which means *to meet by accident* or *to encounter unexpectedly*. (On the other hand, if we say, "The firefighter *ran into* the burning building," the verb is *to run* and the preposition *into* indicates the direction in which the firefighter ran. In this case, there is no phrasal verb, only the standard verb, *to run*, and the preposition, *into*.)

English phrasal verbs are simply an old Germanic way to create verbs. We can see a similar structure in German today. For example, look at the German verb *aufmachen* which means *to open*. If we cut the verb in half, we have *auf* and *machen*. We can put *machen* before the direct object, for example, *die Tür* (the door) and *auf* after the direct object and say, "Er *macht* die Tür *auf*" or "He opens the door." The verb is not *machen*; the verb is *aufmachen*. In the same way, when I say, "John finally *figured* it *out*," the verb is not *to figure*; the verb is *to figure out*, meaning *to solve (for example, a problem) by thinking in logical steps.* The verb *to figure,* by itself, has a different meaning, that is, *to assume* or *to suppose.* ("She wasn't at work, so I *figured* that she was sick. But I was wrong; she was at the beach.")

English has many of these two-word verbs and they pretty much always have synonyms which come from French. Let me give you some examples to illustrate how this can drive English language learners crazy. If I say, "He *put* something *in,*" I mean "He contributed something" (French: contribuer). On the other hand, if I say, "The company *put something out,*" I mean "The company produced something" (French: produire). If I say, "Her comment *put someone out,*" that means "Her comment irritated someone" (French: irriter). So far, so good? If I say, "He *put* them *up,*" that means "He gave them lodging" (French: loger). "He *put* them *up to* the crime" means "He convinced them to commit the crime" (French: convaincre). "He *put up with* them" means "He tolerated them" (French: tolérer). Let's do some more. If I say, "He *put* them *down,*" that means "He insulted them" (French: insulter). "We *put* it *down to* their stupidity or their genius" means "We attributed it to their stupidity or their genius" (French: attribuer). And so on. If you're a non-native speaker and all this *put, put, put* hasn't given you a headache, congratulations!

But it gets worse! Each (Germanic) phrasal verb tends to have a more specific meaning and a more limited usage than its French-origin synonym. For example, compare the phrasal verb "to look up to" and its synonym "to admire" (French: admirer). We can admire people, their actions, or their personal qualities and we can also admire things, such as artwork or even a view from a window. However, we typically only use "to look up to" for 1) *a person* who is still alive, 2) *a person* who is older than we are, and 3) *someone* with whom we have a personal relationship (even if that relationship is only in our mind, with a beloved singer, athlete, writer, etc.). So, while many native speakers may say they admire Lincoln, his character, or his eloquence, they will not

PART NINE

say that they *look up to* him, his character, or his eloquence.

Because phrasal verbs are Germanic, they will, of course, be used more often in speaking and less often in writing than their French-origin synonyms. Yet, phrasal verbs are not slang. English slang words are words which are used in very limited areas of life (for example, medical slang, legal slang, etc.) or words that are used to exclude, such as teenage slang which is meant to exclude the older generation. (Typically, teenage slang is used for only a few years before it's replaced by the slang of the *next* generation of teenagers, excluding the *next* generation of adults.) However, in contrast to slang, phrasal verbs are *not* used by only part of the population and they are *not* a transitory part of the English language. They are some of the oldest verbs in the English language, used by everyone.

In addition, we cannot say that phrasal verbs are *always* "informal" English, as some English language teachers tell their students. Phrasal verbs are used in writing and even in professional or academic situations when they best express an exact idea or image. They are therefore a routine, albeit small, part of professional and academic life. In business, if we write about any kind of reimbursement, such as a salary, we will usually use the French-origin verb *to compensate*. On the other hand, even as professionals, when we are speaking about a personal situation, we are more likely to use the phrasal verb *to make something up to someone*. (For example, a person might say, "We interrupted his speech, so shouldn't we *make it up to* him by giving him more time than the other speakers?")

In other areas of professional and business life, we may *take on* certain responsibilities or we may *point out* something special that we want another person to notice. In science, we *set up* a series of procedures to define what we will do in an experiment, we *carry out* the procedures that we have *set up*, we notice that female rats *make up* 70% of the deceased rats in our experiment, and, finally, we admit that our predictions *turned out* to be right only 45% of the time. If you go into any profession, you'll some times be using phrasal verbs.

I once had a teacher in one of my teaching methodology classes, an American teacher, who said, "I never use phrasal verbs; I tend to be quite formal in my speech." (I made no comment, as I remember.) Hmmm... Did she never *come down with* a bad cold or did nothing ever *come up,* requiring her to ask someone *to fill in for* her? Never *run out of* time, patience, or sugar? Never *straighten out* a misunderstanding or *straighten up* her desk? Never *check out* a new restaurant? You can't speak English fluently without using phrasal verbs.

...

And now for English grammar... It appears to me, after teaching the English language for fifty years, that there are two aspects of English which take an especially long time for non-native English speakers to master. The first one is *phrasal verbs* (which we've just discussed) and the second one is *the present perfect tense,* when we use it for a completed action in the past, as in, "I have said no." It seems that an equivalent to the English present perfect and its way of conceptualizing the past does not exist in any other major language. To native speakers, the present perfect is as normal as breathing, but to non-native speakers, it is weird!

At first glance, I *have said no* appears to be very similar to the French *J'ai dit non,* and the German *Ich habe nein gesagt.* And, in the distant past, it was. (In Old and Middle English, the present perfect was used interchangeably with the simple past.)[64] Then, for reasons which are still unclear, it became more common and, in addition, began to refer to a past action, *not in terms of the time when it took place, but in terms of its impact on the present moment.* In fact, we are now forbidden to attach a specific time to this action! As

PART NINE

soon as we do attach a specific time in the past to the action, in speech or sometimes even in thought, we must switch away from the present perfect and use the simple past.

Think for a moment of the story of Cinderella. When the clock struck midnight, Cinderella's beautiful dress turned into rags and her carriage into a pumpkin. Her beautiful evening was over, done, finished! In the same way, when you're using the English present perfect and you *refer* in any way *to a time in the past*, an imaginary clock strikes and your use of the present perfect is also over, done, finished! There is no way for you to continue with the present perfect. You must now stay in the simple past until you move on to a new idea.

For example, compare two questions, using first the simple past and then the present perfect (to refer to a completed action in the past): "Did you go to Seoul, Korea?" versus "Have you been to Seoul, Korea?" In the question, "Did you go to Seoul?" both the speaker and the listener have *the same approximate time frame in mind* and thus a typical response could be, "Yes, I did. It's a lovely city!" Or "No, I didn't. I came down with the flu and had to stay home." However, when someone asks, "Have you been to Seoul?" *neither the speaker nor the listener is thinking of time;* in fact, the speaker may not remember when the action happened, and the listener may never know when the action took place. The focus is on *the present consequences* of the action. Therefore, a typical answer could be, "Yes, I have. So, when you go to Seoul, I recommend that you visit Traditional Village." Or "No, I haven't. But I hope to go there someday."

Now compare, "I think I lost my keys" and "I think I have lost my keys." In which sentence is my mind going back in time, *imagining the moment in the past* when I wasn't paying attention and left my keys somewhere? In which sentence is my mind focused *on the present consequences* of my action and the fact that *now, at this moment*, I have no key to start my car?

Let's take a quiz (especially for non-native speakers) to see if my explanation has been successful. Which sentence do you think would be a bit better in a job interview? 1) "I *worked* on many projects similar to those which your company handles" or 2) "I've *worked* on many projects similar to those which your company handles." Did you choose the sentence which suggests that these projects belong to your *past* life? Or did you choose the sentence which implies that, because of this work (which took place in the past), *now, at this moment,* you have knowledge which you can apply to a new project? I'm sure you chose the second sentence.

...

There is another verb tense in English which may require non-native speakers to think about time in a new way: the present continuous, which is sometimes called the present progressive. Most English language learners focus on the (correct) idea that we use the present continuous to refer to a continuing action, an action that is happening as we speak. For example, you might ask me, "What are you doing?" and I might answer, "I'm making a cherry-blueberry pie."

However, we can also use the present continuous to describe a long action when we want to highlight its temporary nature or the idea that we have an end to this action in sight. For example, compare these two sentences: "We are living in an apartment on the outskirts of London" and "We live in an apartment on the outskirts of London." Certainly, many people could use either sentence to describe their own situation. However, "We are living in an apartment" suggests that, although this action may end up going on for a long time, *we view it as temporary, not permanent.*

Perhaps we're living in an apartment while we're saving money to buy an affordable house or maybe we have a temporary job assignment in London for a couple of years. In this same situation, however, we could also use the simple present and say, "We live in an apartment." That is, we could simply state where we live, with no implication of an end time for our situation. Since most people either see their living arrangements as long lasting or are not focused on the fact that their arrangements are temporary, they will say "We live in an apartment" much more often than "We are living in an apartment."

So, where did the English present continuous come from? There are various answers. One answer is that French possessed an equivalent structure during the Middle English Period which passed into English and then disappeared from French.[65] Another answer is that, at one point during the Middle English Period, for some unknown reason, English speakers began to say, "He is on walking/He is on singing." Then they began to say, "He is a-walking/ He is a-singing." Finally, they dropped the *a-* and simply said, "He is walking/He is singing." [66] In any case, the daily use of the present continuous is a relatively recent addition to English usage. Shakespeare, innovator that he was, almost never used the present continuous. For example, in *Hamlet*, Prince Hamlet asks Polonius, "What do you read, my lord?" not "What are you reading, my lord?" and, in *Antony and Cleopatra*, Cleopatra asks, "What, goest thou back?" not "What, are you going back?" It would be more than a century after Shakespeare before the use of the present continuous would become widespread.[67]

...

Now let's turn to a final annoying (or quaint, depending on your point of view) aspect of English: irregular verbs. As I discussed in **Part Two**, Old English was a synthetic language, that is, a language which relied on word inflections to communicate meaning. A few of these had already disappeared by the time of the Conquest. Then, between 1250 and 1500, most remaining inflections disappeared. One likely factor is that, as many people left the countryside and moved to the cities, they dropped their remaining inflections, in order to be better understood by other new arrivals from other parts of England.

But consider another possible factor. As the Anglo-French began to learn English, who would be speaking English to them? In many cases, their bilingual English servants. Now, imagine that you were an upper-class Anglo-French man or woman in the 13th or 14th century, with French as your primary language. You probably heard most of the common irregular English verbs again and again: *I am/I was/I have been,* or *I go/I went/I have gone,* etc. So, you could remember those verbs. But when you tried to remember the past tense of less common verbs, such as *to climb* (as in, today I *climb* the hill/yesterday *I clomb* the hill/I *have* often *clomben* the hill), perhaps you didn't remember the correct past tense and what could you do? What *did* you do? Well, maybe you solved your problem by adding *-ed* (which already existed in Old English) [68] and so you said, "I climbed." Perhaps you also added *-ed* to the verb *to laugh* and said, "I laughed," instead of "I low." Everywhere *-ed, -ed, -ed.*

Maybe you could also remember some common irregular nouns, such as one *life*/two *lives,* one *child*/two *children,* and one *tooth*/two *teeth,* but when it came to less common irregular nouns, such as *horse* (plural: *horsen*) or *book* (plural: *beek*), what did you do if you couldn't remember the plural form? I think that you may have just added an *-s*. The *-s* plural ending existed in French as well as in Old English, so why not? [69] And what did bilingual English speakers (your servants, your social inferiors) do when they heard this? Did they correct you? Scold you? Or did they begin to do it themselves?

As I said earlier, most nouns and verbs that are still irregular in English today are the basic words that we repeat over and over in daily life and are therefore likely to be remembered. However, there is another group of words which have retained their irregular endings: words that rarely entered the vocabulary of the French

PART NINE

upper class because they were used in the farm work and fishing that was done by Anglo-Saxons. Some examples of this are *wolf/wolves, sheep/sheep, cow/cattle, ox/oxen, goose/geese, deer/deer, mouse/mice,* and *fish/fish*.[70]

In **Part Ten**, we'll discuss the painful topic of English spelling.

ENTANGLED TONGUES

# PART TEN

## TWELVE PROBLEMS WITH ENGLISH SPELLING

ENTANGLED TONGUES

PART TEN

To understand how we got to the place where we are with English spelling, we need to go far back in time to see that English spelling has always been a problem. From the beginning, the various Anglo-Saxon tribes that arrived in England pronounced and spelled the same words differently. (Problem Number One.) Then, in 597, when Christian missionaries from Italy arrived in England and began to copy the Anglo-Saxon texts, there was another challenge. The Anglo-Saxon writing system used runes, that is, symbols, instead of letters and had at least 37 different sounds. How could the missionaries translate texts which had more than 37 sounds into the Roman alphabet which had only 23 letters? Well, every missionary handled that problem in his own way. (Problem Number Two.) And, beginning in the 8th and 9th centuries, the Vikings added a few of their own words into this linguistic soup. (Minor Problem Number Three.)

Immediately after the Norman Conquest, as official documents were written in Latin and French, there was little interest in English spelling. Later, however, when Anglo-French scribes began to copy the Old English texts, they often added their own French spelling to the Old English words. We've already discussed *hus* which got the Frenchified spelling of *house*. But what about *gest*? What did Anglo-French scribes do with *gest*? Answer: they wrote it as *guest*. Another example of an Old English word with a Frenchified spelling. (Problem Number Four.)

Somehow, the Anglo-French scribes managed to add even more complications. As they copied Old English writings, many scribes used one set of spelling rules for the words which they identified as coming from Latin or French and a different set of rules for Old English words. (Problem Number Five.)

Now this may seem crazy to those of you whose language has logical spelling rules, but apparently this didn't bother the scribes.

36. The scribe at his desk

According to *The Oxford English Dictionary*, there were sixty different ways to spell the word *night* in the 1200s.[71] Law clerks were paid for their writing by the inch, so they would be paid more for spelling *night* as *nieht, nihte,* or *nyhte* than as *nig, nih,* or *nyt*. And they would earn even more for *neghte, nygthe, or nichte*. (Problem Number Six.) This practice went on for many years before Richard Mulcaster denounced it in his *Elementarie* (1582), writing, "If words be overcharged with numbers of letters, that comes by covetousness in such (people) as sell them by lines..."[72]

In 1476, William Caxton brought the first printing press to England. Caxton was a merchant who, in later life, translated literary works from French and printed them, along with works by other writers and translators. In fact, the first book printed in England was Caxton's own translation of a French book. (More

PART TEN

than a third of Caxton's output consisted of French writings, which he printed in French, or translations from French).[73] It seems that, when he printed works in English, Caxton allowed a variety of spellings; he tended to print whatever was in the original manuscript. However, if one line in the final printed version was shorter than the others, he sometimes added extra letters to make the spacing look more consistent. For example, Caxton often added an *-e* at the end of a word which had not had one before, so we see the word *English* spelled as *Englyssh* or, in some cases, *Englysshe*. (Problem Number Seven.)

Caxton had been using a printing press in Belgium before he returned to England and so he brought back a few Belgian printers with him, including Wynkyn de Worde, who spoke Dutch and probably very little English. Clearly, these printers saw that their boss was flexible about spelling and so, when Caxton printed *Royal Book* in 1484 and referred to the Christian Trinity (Father, Son, and Holy Ghost), the Old English word for *ghost*, that is, *gost*, was suddenly spelled *ghoost*, similar to the Dutch *gheest*.

37. Caxton presents his printing press to the King and Queen

We see *ghoost* again when Caxton printed Chaucer's *Book of Fame*. In the 1549 edition of *The Book of Common Prayer*, we still see the *Holy Gost* but, a few years later, in Shakespeare's play, Hamlet's father got an *-h* and became a *ghost*. Caxton's spellings of goose as *ghoose*, goat as *ghoot*, and girl as *gherle* did not survive, but *aghast* and *ghastly* are still with us today. (Problem Number Eight, thanks to Wynkyn de Worde et al.)

I've just said that William Caxton was flexible about spelling and that's true, but he was only somewhat flexible. Because Caxton set up his printing press just outside London, near the Chancery in Westminster, his use of English tended to mirror the Chancery Standard, following its usage close to 90% of the time. [74] Both his English and Chancery English reflected the London/East Midlands dialect, which was somewhere between the southern Old English dialect and the northern Norse dialect. We therefore see Caxton sometimes choosing to use an Old English word and, at other times, choosing to use a Norse word when he translated French works into English.*

There is a well-known story that Caxton told about his work as a translator. At one time, he was translating a work from French and was not sure how to translate the French word *oeuf* (which means *egg*). To illustrate his dilemma, he told the story of a merchant from the north of England who was visiting the south of England and asked a woman if he could buy the eggs that she was selling. The merchant used the Norse word *egges*. The woman indicated that she couldn't understand him, insisting that she didn't speak French. The merchant became angry. Luckily, a man nearby saw the problem and, using the Old English word, he asked the woman if the merchant could buy her *eyren*. Finally, the woman understood, and the merchant got his eggs. In the end, Caxton decided to use the Norse word *egges*, instead of the Anglo-Saxon *eyren*, in his translation. So, today we, too, use the Norse word *egges*, and not *eyren*.**

# PART TEN

This anecdote helps us to understand why a few English words today are so similar to Norwegian or Danish words (that is, Norse words) and so different from the equivalent German words: for example, the English *egg*, the Norwegian *egg*, and the Danish *aeg* versus the German *ei*. On the other hand, many English words are very similar to German words and very different from the equivalent Norwegian or Danish words: for example, the English *I speak* and the German *Ich spreche* versus the Norwegian *jeg snakker* and the Danish *jeg taler*. (Problem Number Nine.)

There were also writers who insisted on updating English spelling to accommodate the continuing influx of French words. For example, the Old English word *build* was usually spelled *bild* or *byld*, but with the arrival of the French words *guild* and *guilt*, writers began to add the letter *-u* to *bild* and *bilt* in order to harmonize *build* with *guild* and *built* with *guilt*. (Problem Number Ten.)

In 1695, the anonymous author of *The Writing Scholar's Companion* wrote that, "silent consonants... must be written" in all words which originally came from Latin. [75] So, the French-origin word *dette* began to be spelled as *debt* to show that it had originally come from the Latin word *debitum*. In the same way, *doubt* got its *-b* to show that, before it moved into French and then into English, it had existed as the Latin word *dubius*. *Diplome* got an *-a* and became *diploma*. *Auteur* got an *-h* and became *author*. *Receipt* got its *-p*, *reign* got a *-g*, and *adventure* got its *-d*. And so on. All of a sudden, *anonyme* became *anonymous*. And although the word *island* did not come from Latin, but from the Old English word *igland*, it still got an *-s* to Latinize it! (Problem Number Eleven.)

To make matters worse, just as Henry V, the Chancery and Caxton were managing to create some standards of English spelling and usage, The Great Vowel Shift occurred, 1400 to 1600. With the Great Vowel Shift, the pronunciation of the English vowels (a, e, i, o, u) shifted and English spelling became even more unconnected to English pronunciation than before. (Think of the *ou* sound in the words *cough, enough, though, through,* and *plough.*) Why did The Great Vowel Shift occur? Historians are not sure. Many researchers cite the movement of people from all over England to the larger cities, creating competition between the various regional pronunciations. This was certainly a factor.

But could another (possibly small) factor be that, between 1400 and 1600, some (bilingual) French speakers were giving a French pronunciation to English words and that some (bilingual) English speakers were giving an English pronunciation to French words that had entered into English? In any case, English spelling became somewhat standardized, just before this huge change in English pronunciation. Which means that our spelling today tends to reflect the pre-Great Vowel Shift pronunciation and not our actual post-Great Vowel Shift pronunciation. (Problem Number Twelve.)

I could go on, but you've probably gotten the point. If you'd like to learn more about English spelling, I recommend the very readable and entertaining book *Spell It Out* by David Crystal which summarizes a huge amount of research on English spelling and, in 328 pages, should answer most of your questions.

So, how can the average person make sense of English spelling? You probably can't, unless you devote much of your life to this subject. However, one thing that you can do is to learn English spelling rules, such as "*i* before *e*, except after *c*." But wait! What about: *eight, neighbor, weight, weird, seize, science,* and so on? OK, better yet, 1) read a lot and pay attention to the spelling of new words, 2) study lists of the commonly misspelled English words, and 3) get Spell Check on your computer. There is a reason why almost every native English speaker has Spell Check.

On the other hand, ...

*I have a spelling checker; it came with my PC*

# PART TEN

*It plane lee marks four my revue*

*Miss steaks aye can knot sea.*

*Eye ran this poem threw it;*

*Your sure reel glad two no.*

*Its vary polished in it's way.*

*My checker tolled me sew.*

By Mark Eckman and Jerold Zar

In **Part Eleven**, we'll look at the result of all that we've discussed so far: Modern English.

---

\* In the same way that Chaucer not only inserted French vocabulary into his own English works but also retained some of the French vocabulary when he translated French works into English, Caxton also sometimes kept the original French word when he translated French texts into English and then printed them. This illustrates another way in which French vocabulary entered into English during this time.

\*\* Norse will win this competition between its *-s* plural ending and the Old English *-en* plural ending, as we saw in Caxton's story of the Norse *egges* versus the Anglo-Saxon *eyren*. Today the Old English *-en* plural ending has virtually disappeared, with a few exceptions, such as *child/children*, *man/men*, and *woman/women*.

ENTANGLED TONGUES

# PART ELEVEN

MODERN ENGLISH,
1500 TO THE PRESENT

ENTANGLED TONGUES

PART ELEVEN

The year 1500 is usually given as the date that marks the end of the turbulent transitional Middle English period and the birth of Modern English, the language that we speak today. That is, by 1500, the merger of French and Germanic dialects in England was essentially complete. English, or the new *Frenglish,* as some might describe it, was acknowledged as the national language of England and French took on a new, lesser role as an optional language of communication and an optional source of vocabulary.

In that year, 1500, the king of England was Henry VII, the first of the Tudor line of kings (who would all descend from Catherine de Valois, the widow of Henry V, and her second husband Owen Tudor). Henry VII married an English wife as had done the previous two kings, Richard III (the last of the Plantagenet line of kings) and Richard III's predecessor Edward IV. By the late 1400s and early 1500s, English kings no longer expected to marry a French wife who would bring large numbers of French-speaking relatives, supporters, and hangers-on to the English court. Future queens (and queen consorts) would come either from England or from a number of other countries.

In 1509, Henry VIII, whom you might remember for his six wives ("Divorced, beheaded, died, divorced, beheaded, survived") began his reign as a 17-year-old king. Unlike his father, Henry VIII dreamed that he might repeat the triumphs of Henry V, but his efforts came to nothing more than a few battles on French soil.

An embarrassing incident occurred in 1520. Henry VIII reconciled for a time with the king of France and accepted the king's invitation to the legendary Field of Cloth of Gold. At one point, Henry's herald started to read, "I, Henry, by the grace of God, King of England and France…," using the same form that every English king had employed since the time of Edward III.

38. The Field of Cloth of Gold

Henry hurriedly stopped his herald and apologized to King Francis, insisting that he was simply "Henry, King of England." [76] Two years later, after he made another attempt to invade France, the English people indicated their unwillingness to finance a third effort and so, for some time, Henry had to give up the idea of becoming king of France. During the next few years, he was forced to content himself with chatting in French to the many French visitors to his court and writing love letters in French to Anne Boleyn.

39. Henry VIII

PART ELEVEN

40. Anne Boleyn

And now that we have brought up the subject of Anne Boleyn, let's look at the influence that she had on English. Anne Boleyn is not someone that we think of as a champion of the English language. She had spent seven years in France, from the age of 14 to 21, as a maid of honor and companion to the French queen Claude (who was only two years older than Anne), before she returned to England where she was noted for her perfect French, her French fashions, and her French mannerisms. When Henry VIII left his first wife, Catherine, in order to marry Anne in 1534, the Catholic pope threatened to excommunicate him. Henry's response was to reject Catholicism and to turn to Protestantism, which, of course, has no Pope.

Since Protestants believed that the Bible should be printed in the language of the people, Henry's initial hostility to printing the Bible in English was softened. His change in attitude came too late to save William Tyndale from being burned at the stake for translating the Bible into English. However, the next year, in 1537, the Matthews Bible, based largely on Tyndale's work, received permission to be printed in England and, in 1539, the Great Bible became the first authorized translation of the Bible into English.

Henry's daughter by Anne Boleyn was Queen Elizabeth I (1533-1603), who did not make a claim to the French throne; she was more interested in manipulating the French to serve her own purposes than in fighting them. While she honored the memory of Henry V, Elizabeth had no desire to refight the Hundred Years War. Instead, the "Elizabethan Age," as we call this time, is remembered primarily as a golden age of peace, prosperity, and great achievements in art, music, and literature. And, when we think of the Elizabethan Age, the first name that usually comes to mind is that of the poet and playwright William Shakespeare.

41. William Shakespeare

Shakespeare, of course, is known for his skill at tapping into the emotional (and political?) power of Anglo-Saxon speech. For example, in the play *Henry V*, before he leads his soldiers into battle, Henry V speaks to them in this way: (See if you can spot the only French-origin word that he uses.)

## PART ELEVEN

In his plays, Shakespeare uses not only French words, but also French sentence structures which sound odd to an English ear. For example, he repeatedly uses an *or...*, *or...* structure, which echoes the common French *ou ...*, *ou...* and *soit...*, *soit...* structures, instead of the standard English, *either...*, *or...* (as we see in *Antony and Cleopatra*, when Antony says, "*Or* I will live, *Or* bathe my dying honor in the blood").

In *Henry V*, Shakespeare writes much of an entire scene in French in which the daughter of the French king, Catherine of Valois, is learning English from her lady-in-waiting. Later in the play, much of another scene is also in French, when Henry V (who in real life spoke fluent French) woos Catherine in broken French. Now, Queen Elizabeth's court was full of men and women who had learned French at an early age, had spent time in France, wrote poetry in French, and translated French works (as she did). Clearly, Shakespeare wrote with the bilingual English court in mind and believed that these scenes would make them laugh.*

Finally, in his sonnets, Shakespeare, at times, copies the themes and even the language of the French poets of his time. For example, how can I hear, "*Your monument shall be my gentle verse, which eyes not yet created shall o'er-read... You still shall live, such virtue hath my pen*" without remembering earlier lines by Pierre de Ronsard (1524-1585)? Also visualizing future generations of readers, Ronsard wrote "*Donne moy l'encre et le papier aussi... cent papiers plus durs que diamant...*" and "*Vous vivrez... tant que vivront les plumes et le livre.*" ("Give me ink and paper, too... a hundred papers harder than diamonds..." and "You shall live... as long as shall live pens and books.")

Now compare my translation (almost word for word) of one of Ronsard's observations to the lines that Shakespeare puts into the mouth of his character Jaques in the play *As You Like It*. Ronsard: "*Le monde est le théâtre, et les hommes acteurs... La Fortune apreste les habitz...En gestes differens, en differens langages, Roys, Princes, et Bergers jouent leurs personnages."* My translation: *"The world is a theatre and mankind the actors... Fortune lends the costumes... with different gestures and different languages, kings, princes and shepherds all play their parts."* Shakespeare's lines: *"All the world's a stage, And all the men and women merely players. They have their exits and their entrances, and one man in his time plays many parts."*

Queen Elizabeth I, who spoke perfect French, loved Ronsard's poetry and could recite many of his poems by heart. (Famous as a penny-pincher, she once sent him a diamond!) I wonder if she smiled in recognition upon hearing Shakespeare's reworking of Ronsard's images.

I'm told that, to understand Shakespeare, it's useful to have a knowledge of Middle English, the Geneva Bible, Ovid, Plutarch, Elizabethan law, medicine, botany, falconry and more.** Perhaps we should add a knowledge of French to this list...

Another aspect of Shakespeare's writing, which easily goes unnoticed today, is his use of *thou* and *thee*. In Old English, *you* was always plural, always used to speak to multiple people, whereas *thou* (direct object *thee*) was always singular, always used to speak to only one person. In the 1200s, English speakers started to use *you* and *thou* in the same way that French speakers use *vous* and *tu*. From then on, the English word *you* was used, like the French *vous,* not only to address multiple people, but also as a polite way to address only one person.[77] On the other hand, the English *thou*, still used to speak to only one person, acquired the connotation of familiarity which we experience in the French *tu*. By the time that Shakespeare wrote, most English people had dropped the familiar *thou* and only used the polite *you*.[78] Shakespeare and his characters, however, were clearly at ease with this distinction and used it for dramatic effect.

Going back to Shakespeare's play *Twelfth Night*, we meet again the Lady Olivia who has fallen in love with Cesario (who is

## PART ELEVEN

actually a woman who has been shipwrecked and feels compelled, for her own safety, to disguise herself as a man). Lady Olivia hides her feelings and always uses the formal *you* with Cesario, until, one day, as she sees that he is leaving, she cries out, "Stay!... Tell me what *thou* think'st of me." By using *thou* instead of *you*, Lady Olivia is opening her heart to Cesario and is waiting to see if Cesario will also use the familiar *thou*. But Cesario responds with the formal *you*. Lady Olivia stiffens up, takes control of her feelings, and begins to use *you* again. However, she soon loses her self-control and confesses her love, saying, "I love *thee* so."

42. *Twelfth Night*

Cesario tries to re-establish an emotional distance by using *you* once more, insisting "no woman... shall mistress be of... my heart." (Don't worry; there will be a happy ending when her twin brother Sebastian arrives, and "Cesario" is able to reveal that she is a woman, which leads to a double wedding.) In any case, this back-and-forth between *you* and *thou* goes over the heads of most English speakers today; they no longer respond emotionally, as their ancestors did, to a sudden switch from *you* to *thou* or from *thou* to *you*.\*\*\*/\*\*\*\*

From Shakespeare's time on, the role of the French language in England continued to diminish. In 1714, the childless Queen

Anne died, and the crown passed to her second cousin, George of Hanover in Germany, who spoke German, French, and very little English. (From then on, until the 20th century, all English monarchs would speak German and marry Germanic spouses.) George I's grandson George III became the first of the Hanoverians to speak English as his first language. His granddaughter, who became Queen Victoria, was born in May 1819, soon after her parents hurried from Germany to England to ensure that their baby would be in line for the throne. As Queen, Victoria spoke English to her subjects, German to her husband, Prince Albert (even when they had company, which offended many people), and French to visiting royalty and diplomats. During World War I, her grandson, George V would change the name of the royal family from Hanover to Windsor, its current name.

Despite the reduced influence of French at the English court, 19th century English writers continued to assume that educated readers would understand French. In Charlotte Bronte's famous novel, *Jane Eyre* (probably the least French of her novels), the two main characters, Jane Eyre and Mr. Rochester, use French phrases repeatedly in their conversations. Their connection to each other is a little French girl who goes back and forth between French and English. Bronte refused to give any translations for her French dialogues; clearly, she believed that her readers *should* understand.

## PART ELEVEN

Other 19th century British writers who brought their love of French into their works were Charles Dickens, William Makepeace Thackery, and Oscar Wilde who wrote a complete play, *Salomé*, in French. Anthony Trollope and the Scottish novelist Margaret Oliphant (who was said to be Queen Victoria's favorite writer*****) also scattered French phrases and expressions throughout their novels (*ce n'est que le premier pas qui coûte,* to be *de trop, faute de mieux,* etc.), apparently agreeing with Charlotte Bronte that their readers should and would understand.******

On the other hand, another 19th century writer, Jane Austen, disapproved of inserting foreign words into English novels; French words or references are put into the mouths of her most annoying and/or pretentious characters. Thus, Mrs. Elton and Anne Steele boast of their *beaux*, the silly Mrs. Bennett can't get over the idea that Mr. Darcy may have two French cooks, and, in *Sanditon,* the vain Sir Edward glories in his *cottage orné*.

Have you heard the expression, "Pardon my French?" If I break my favorite china teacup, and you hear me whisper one of the (milder) Old English four-letter words, perhaps I will quickly add, "Pardon my French," meaning "Pardon my bad language." However, the original meaning of this phrase is very different from its current meaning. In the 19th century, people in England commonly used French words and phrases in their conversations and would apologize, in advance, for any mistakes that they might make. Why did they feel the need to apologize? Because... 900 years after the Norman Conquest, there was still a tendency in England to equate the ability to speak French with a high level of education. Therefore, to make a mistake in French was to signal a defect in one's education.

Finally, what about the 20th and 21st centuries?

44. British passport 2020

Today, although French is very much a foreign language in England, it is still taught from early childhood to those in line for the throne. And, even now, when a bill becomes law, the clerk of the House of Lords announces in French, "Le roy le veult" or "La reyne le veult" ("The king wishes it" or "The Queen wishes it"), using French phrases that have been used in the English parliament for hundreds of years. On British passports, we still see the defiant "Dieu et mon droit" ("God and my right") as well as "Honi soit qui mal y pense" ("Shame on those who think bad of it"). Why are these phrases on British passports? Well, "Dieu et mon droit" was the battle cry of Richard the Lionheart in the 12th century and "Honi soit qui mal y pense" goes back to King Edward III, speaking to save the dignity of a lady (his cousin) at a ball during the Hundred Years War. These phrases were the speech of English kings.

In **Part Twelve,** we'll revisit questions raised in **Part One**.

PART ELEVEN

* To the north, French was also spoken in the court of Elizabeth's cousin, Mary, Queen of Scots. After the death of her father, James V, little Mary was raised by her French mother (in hiding from Henry VIII) until, at age five, she was spirited to the safety of the French court. There she was celebrated for her beauty by the poet Ronsard who, years later and still in touch with both Mary, and Elizabeth, would beg Queen Elizabeth to be merciful to Mary during her captivity, writing, "Royne, qui enfermez une Royne si rare, Adoucissez vostre ire et changez de conseil," ("Queen, you who imprison a Queen so rare, Soften your anger and change your mind"). As Mary's biographer Stefan Zweig notes, even after Mary returned to Scotland at age 18, French was the language of her conversations, her thoughts, and her poetry. Her passionate letters to Bothwell, the (recently discovered) encrypted letters that she wrote during her captivity, and the only letter that she wrote the night before Elizabeth had her beheaded, were in French.

** As a native English speaker (although I prefer the original English version), I find it easier to understand a Shakespeare play in French than in English. How can that be? Let me give you two examples, with the first example from *Othello*. "If I do prove her haggard/ Though that her jesses were my dear heartstrings/I'd whistle her off and let her down the wind." This is the language of falconry, the sport of kings, and so I, being no king, needed to learn some of the language of falconry to understand these lines. Now look at the fine French translation: "Si je la trouve rebelle à ma voix, quand les liens qui l'attachent à moi seraient les fibres mêmes de mon coeur, je la repousserai en sifflant et je l'abandonnerai au vent..." A native English speaker who has taken a few French classes can understand the French version and yet be baffled by the original English version. In *Hamlet*, Rosencrantz speaks of "an eyrie of children, little eyases..." Most adult English speakers have no idea that that an "eyrie" is the nest of a bird of prey and that "eyases" is a term for baby falcons or hawks. On the other hand, the French "une nichée d'enfants, de petjts bec-jaunes" is easily understood by French children. I suspect that my examples hold for translations into other languages as well...

\*\*\* Sometime during the 16th century, for reasons unknown, London area writers began to replace the Old English (3rd person singular) *-eth* verb ending with the northern Norse *-s* ending. (*He maketh* was replaced by *he makes*, etc.) Caxton never used the *-s* verb ending in his printing,[79] but, a few years later, the *-s* ending appeared in Shakespeare's works. Sometimes Shakespeare used both endings in the same sentence, as when he wrote in *The Merchant of Venice*:

*The quality of mercy is not strain'd.*
*It <u>droppeth</u> as the gentle rain from heaven*
*Upon the place beneath. It is twice blest:*
*It <u>blesseth</u> him that <u>gives</u>, and him that <u>takes</u>.*

Although *The King James* version of the *Bible* was written *after* Shakespeare's works, it was faithful to the Old English *-eth* ending.

\*\*\*\* Most people would agree that Shakespeare's works and the *King James Bible* (1611) represent the height of English literature. However, these works represent very different approaches to the English language. Shakespeare is known for the many new words, often French, that he introduced in his plays and poetry. On the other hand, about 80% of the *King James Bible* (with its s*pake* for *spoke*, *gat* for *got*, and *ye* for *you*, etc.) is taken from Tyndale's Bible, written in the early 1500s, which includes much of Wycliffe's older translation. In sum, Shakespeare *innovated* while the King James Bible *preserved*.

\*\*\*\*\* In Oliphant's novel *May*, her themes of enduring grief, the heavy constraints of 19th century duty and morality, and the beauty of Scottish landscape and meteorology would surely have resonated with Queen Victoria.

\*\*\*\*\*\* These novelists reflect differing views of the role of French in 19th century Britain. Some, such as Trollope and Oliphant (who wore their French so lightly), clearly viewed French as an integral part of British linguistic heritage and an invaluable source of nuanced words and expressions. Charles Dickens, however, seemed to view French very much as an arbiter of social standing; his characters take French lessons only to increase their social status. Dickens, too, studied French as an adult and his subsequent competence served, no doubt, as reassurance that he, like Pip in his *Great Expectations*, had left behind his socially and financially precarious childhood and had achieved the status of gentleman (*gentilhomme*).

# PART TWELVE

## CONCLUSION

ENTANGLED TONGUES

PART TWELVE

When I was growing up, I learned that the past of *to dream* was *dreamt*, the past of *to leap* was *leapt*, and the past of *to shine* was *shone*. Today it seems that almost everyone says, "I dreamed" or "I leaped," with an *-ed* ending. OK. But when I hear someone say that the light *shined*, instead of *shone*, I think, "Can't we keep just this one lovely Old English irregular verb?" The answer, of course, is no. Just as English speakers hundreds of years ago felt the need to add an *-s* to Old English irregular nouns and an *-ed* to Old English irregular verbs, today many people are happy to say, "I leaped at the chance" instead of "I leapt at the chance." It seems that this momentum, which began almost a thousand years ago, will continue and that, in the future, more and more Old English irregular nouns and verbs will end up with shiny new *-s* and *-ed* endings.

The English vocabulary, too, continues to evolve. When I was at school in New Zealand (more than half a century ago now), before classes each morning, the girls would assemble outside the classrooms and, under the watchful eye (and commentary!) of the headmistress, recite a pledge of loyalty to the Queen and the Commonwealth. I have forgotten this pledge, except for the words "our awful Queen Elizabeth." Of course, when the pledge was first written, the word *awful* meant *awe-inspiring*, that is, a positive term of deep respect for the queen. However, even in the 1960s, that meaning was remote enough that a few girls would giggle as they said it. Today who would say it at all?

As just one more example, in the 19$^{th}$ century, *wonderful* did not have the very positive meaning that it has today. It simply meant *inspiring wonder* or *great surprise* and could be used in a sentence such as "It was *wonderful* that the charming Willoughby turned out to be such a heartless villain." (Something to keep in mind when we read 19$^{th}$ century novels.) If you and I are ever able to time travel to the future, we will certainly find people a few hundred years from now, who will find our way of speaking just as strange as we find the English that was spoken only a few hundred years ago...

So, how can we summarize our discussion of the influence of French on English?

The existential drama of the English language began in 1066 when the French language arrived in England as *an imposed language*, that is, the language of the newly created Norman ruling class. Then, for several centuries, we see a kind of peaceful co-existence, with French words steadily moving into English as *a replacement language*, providing substitute words for the Old English vocabulary that had been lost and also providing a huge number of synonyms for the Old English words which survived. Today, however, the French language serves as a source of *optional vocabulary*, used by only a (smaller and smaller) subset of the population.

As a result of this centuries-long drama, 1) English grammar became a mixture of French and Germanic structures, 2) English spelling became an even bigger headache, and 3) the size of the English vocabulary exploded. As English lost its inflections and its identity as a synthetic language, the role of word order and prepositions became crucial to establishing the meaning of a sentence. That is, English became an analytic language. And, as an analytic language, without the need to create new inflections for each new word, it became much easier for English to accept words from other languages, as it has done enthusiastically.

The result of all this, Modern English, is a language which is known for its huge vocabulary and its enormous number of synonyms, each word with its own distinct shade of meaning. In short, this merger, this *Frenglish*, this marriage of French and (Germanic) Old English, has produced a language *which works*, often beautifully, even if it drives us crazy sometimes.

# PART TWELVE

In Part One, I hinted at three questions: Why this enormous vocabulary? Why this grammar? And why this spelling? I hope you understand now why there are wonderful *and long* books which answer these questions in much more detail than I've done and why the best short answer to these questions may simply be that English is "a hodgepodge of all other speeches."

I raised another question early in the book: how did English evolve, within a few hundred years, from a synthetic language with a rich Germanic vocabulary to an analytic language with more words of French origin than of Germanic origin? I hope that I have answered that question as well.

Which leads us to the one question that I raised in **Part One** which I leave for you to answer: how should we conceptualize this story of the English language? Is the story of English essentially *a heroic comeback story*, the story of a language which suffered an enormous shock, miraculously survived, and ended up producing some of the greatest literature that the world has ever known?

Or, as Cerquiglini suggests, should English, as an analytic language, with a predominantly French and Latin vocabulary, now be classified as a Romance language, rather than as a Germanic language? If so, is the story of English the saga of *its journey from one linguistic family to another linguistic family, losing much along the way, but ultimately gaining even more?*

Of course, everyone has his or her own opinion. According to the British historian, E.A. Freeman (1823-1892): *"This abiding corruption of our language, I believe to have been the one result of the Norman Conquest which has been purely evil."* [80]

Et puis voilà. There you have it.

ENTANGLED TONGUES

# Bibliography

Allmand, Christopher. 1992. *Henry V*. Berkeley and Los Angeles: University of California.

Barber, Charles. 2000. *The English Language: A Historical Introduction*. Cambridge: Cambridge University Press.

Bennett, Michael. 1999. *Richard II and the Revolution of 1399*. Somerset: Sutton.

Boüard, Michel de. 1984. *Guillaume le Conquérant*. Paris: Fayard

Bouet, Pierre. 2021. *Hastings 14 octobre 1066*. Paris: Tallandier.

Bragg, Melvyn. 2003. *The Adventure of English:* New York: Arcade.

Brie, Friedrich. 1906. *The Brut; or, The Chronicles of England*. London: Early English Text Society.

Butterfield, Ardis. 1986. "Chaucer's French Inheritance." In *The Cambridge Companion to Chaucer*, by Piero Boitani and Jill Mann, 20-35. Cambridge: Cambridge University Press.

Cable, Albert C. Baugh and Thomas. 2002. *A History of the English Language*. Upper Saddle River: Pearson Education.

Cerquiglini, Bernard. 2024. *"La langue anglaise n'existe pas" C'est du français mal prononcé*. Paris: Gallimard.

Claiborne, Robert. 1983. *Our Marvelous Native Tongue:* New York: The New York Times Book Co.

Crystal, David. 2013. *Spell It Out*. New York: St. Martin's Press.

Fisher, John H. 1996. *The Emergence of Standard English*. Lexington: The University Press of Kentucky.

Freeman, Edward A. 1876. *The History of the Norman Conquest of England*, vol 5. Oxford: Clarendon Press.

Hanley, Catherine. 2016. *Louis: The French Prince Who Invaded England*. New Haven: Yale University Press.

—. 2022. *Two Houses Two Kingdoms: A History of France and England 1100-1300*. New Haven: Yale University Press

Harrison, William. 1577. Reprinted 1968. *The Description of England*. Ithaca: Cornell University Press.

Howarth, David. 1977. *1066*. New York: Penguin.

Ingham, Richard. 2014. "The Maintenance of French in Later Medieval England." *Neuphilologische Mitteilungen,* vol.115, no.4, 425-48.

Jones, Terry. 2003. *Who Murdered Chaucer? A Medieval Mystery*. New York: St. Martins Press.

Kelly, Amy. 1978. *Eleanor of Aquitaine and the Four Kings*. Cambridge: Harvard University Press.

Kibbee, Douglas A. 1991. *For To Speke Frenche Trewly: The French Language in England, 1000-1600*. Philadelphia: Benjamins

Le Héricher, Édouard. 1918. *L'Histoire de la Langue Anglaise, Introduction*. Reprinted Wentworth Press, 2018

Lusignan, Serge. 2004. *La langue des rois au Moyen Age*. Paris: Presses Universitaires de France.

Michaelis, Laura. "The Ambiguity of the English Present Perfect," *Journal of Linguistics,* vol. 30, no.1, 111-157

Millward, C.M. 1988. *A Biography of the English Language*. New York: Harcourt Brace Jovanovich.

Omrod, W.M. 2003. "The Use of English: Language, Law, and Political Culture in Fourteenth-Century England." *Speculum,* vol.78, no.3: 750-787.

Orr, John. 1962. *Old French and Modern English Idiom*. Oxford: Basil Blackwell & Mott, LTD.

Rex, Peter. 2011. *1066: A New History of the Norman Conquest*. Gloucester: Amberley Publishing.

Robinson, Fred. 2004. "The History of English and Its Practical Uses." *The Swanee Review,* vol 112. no 3, 376-395.

Short, Ian. 1980. "On Bilingualism in Anglo-Norman England." *Romance Philology,* vol.33, no.4, May, 1980: 467-479.

St. Aubyn. 1991. *Queen Victoria: A Portrait.* New York: Atheneum

Suggett, Helen. 1946. "Use of French in the Later Middle Ages." *Transactions of the Royal Historical Society,* vol 28, 61-83.

Trotter, David. 2003. "L'Anglo-Normand: Variété Insulaire ou Variété Isolée." *Médiévals,* no. 45, 43-54.

Walter, Henriette. 2001. *Honni soit qui mal y pense.* Paris: Éditions Robert Laffont.

Warner, Kathryn. 2017. *Richard II: A True King's Fall.* Gloucester: Amberley.

Weir, Alison. 2008. *Henry VIII: The King and His Court.* New York: Ballantine.

—. 2022. *Queens of the Age of Chivalry.* New York: Ballantine.

Wendover, Roger of. 1236. Printed 1849. *Flowers of History,* vol. I. and II. London: Henry G. Bohn.

Williams, Deanne. 2004. *The French Fetish from Chaucer to Shakespeare.* Cambridge: Cambridge University Press.

Zweig, Stefan. 1933. *Marie Stuart.* Paris: Éditions Bernard Grasset

# Endnotes

[1] Claiborne, *Our Marvelous Tongue*, 5

[2] Williams, *The French Fetish from Chaucer to Shakespeare*, 182

[3] Baugh, *A History of the English Language*, 104

[4] Baugh, *A History of the English Language*, 99

[5] Baugh, *A History of the English Language*, 105

[6] Baugh, *A History of the English Language*, 67

[7] Lusignan, *La Langue des rois au Moyen Age*, 210

[8] Bouet, *Hastings: 14 octobre 1066*, 49

[9] Williams, *The French Fetish from Chaucer to Shakespeare*, 6

[10] Wendover, *Flowers of History, vol. I*, 371

[11] Rex, *1066*, 98

[12] Lusignan, *La Langue des rois au Moyen Age*, 167

[13] Lounsbury, *History of the English Language*, 175

[14] Barber, *The English Language: A Historical Introduction*, 177

[15] Lusignan, *La Langue des rois au Moyen Age*, 159

[16] Howarth, *1066: The Year of the Conquest*, 198

[17] Harrison, *The Description of England*, 415

[18] Claiborne, *Our Marvelous Tongue*, 107

[19] Kelly, *Eleanor of Aquitaine and the Four Kings*, 173

[20] Baugh, *A History of the English Language*, 168

[21] Baugh, *A History of the English Language*, 55

[22] Baugh, *A History of the English Language*, 115

[23] Robinson, "History of English and Its Practical Uses," 388

[24] Suggett, "The Use of French in England in the Later Middle Ages," 71-78

[25] Ingham, "The Maintenance of French in Later Medieval England," 429-432

[26] Short, Ian. (2009) "L'Anglo-Normand au siècle de Chaucer: un regain de statistiques." In Claire Kappler and Suzanne Thiolier-Méjean (eds.), *Le plurilinguisme au Moyen Age Orient/ Occident*, 67–77. Paris: Harmattan. Cited in Ingham, "The Maintenance of French in Later Medieval England," 442

[27] Wendover, *Flowers of History, vol. II*, 555-568

[28] Hanley, *Louis: The French Prince Who Invaded England*, 177

[29] Baugh, *A History of the English Language*, 129

[30] Weir, *Queens of the Age of Chivalry*, 348

[31] Baugh, *A History of the English Language*, 150-151

[32] Williams, *The French Fetish from Chaucer to Shakespeare*, 10

[33] Omrod, "The Use of English: Language, Law, and Political Culture," 781

[34] Milward, *A Biography of the English Language*, 174

[35] Trotter, "L'Anglo-Normand: Variété Insulaire ou Variété Isolée," 49

[36] Suggett, "The Use of French in England in the Later Middle Ages," 67

[37] Hanley, *Louis: The French Prince Who Invaded England*, 247

[38] Ingham, "The Maintenance of French in Later Medieval England," 443

[39] Bragg, *The Adventure of the English Language*, 61

[40] Williams, *The French Fetish from Chaucer to Shakespeare*, 21

[41] Le Héricher, *L'Histoire de la Langue Anglaise, Introduction*, 42

[42] Butterfield, "Chaucer's French Inheritance," 34

[43] Fisher, *The Emergence of Standard English*, 107

[44] Warner, *Richard II: A True King's Fall*, 282

[45] Jones, *Who Murdered Chaucer? A Medieval Mystery*, 5

[46] Jones, *Who Murdered Chaucer? A Medieval Mystery*, 35

[47] Bragg, *The Adventure of the English Language*, 64

[48] Lusignan, *La Langue des rois au Moyen Age*, 202

[49] Baugh, *A History of the English Language*, 151

[50] Brie, *The Brut, or The Chronicles of England*, 545

[51] Jones, *Who Murdered Chaucer? A Medieval Mystery*, 270-271

[52] Kibbee, *For to Speke Frenche Trewly*, 110

[53] Walter, *Honnni soit qui mal y pense*, 152

[54] Walter, *Honnni soit qui mal y pense*, 12

[55] Baugh, *A History of the English Language*, 178

[56] Barber, *The English Language: A Historical Introduction*, 145

[57] Milward, *A Biography of the English Language*, 173

[58] Baugh, *A History of the English Language*, 179

[59] Cerquiqlini, *La langue anglaise n'existe pas*, 53

[60] Cerquiqlini, *La langue anglaise n'existe pas*, 55

[61] Walter, *Honnni soit qui mal y pense*, 97

[62] Orr, *Old French and Modern English Idiom*, V

[63] Claiborne, *Our Marvelous Tongue*, 70

[64] Visser, F.T. (1963) *An Historical Syntax of the English Language*. Cited in Michaelis, "The Ambiguity of the English Present Perfect," 115

[65] Cerquiqlini, *La langue anglaise n'existe pas*, 55-56

[66] Baugh, *A History of the English Language*, 292

[67] Baugh, *A History of the English Language*, 291

[68] Baugh, *A History of the English Language*, 51

[69] Baugh, *A History of the English Language*, 159-160

[70] Milward, *A Biography of the English Language*, 173

[71] Crystal, *Spell It Out*, 110

[72] Crystal, *Spell It Out*, 11

[73] Williams, *The French Fetish from Chaucer to Shakespeare*, 92

[74] Fisher, *The Emergence of Standard English*, 129

[75] Crystal, *Spell It Out*, 154

[76] Weir, *Henry VIII*, 224

[77] Lounsbury, *History of the English Language*, 287

[78] Lounsbury, *History of the English Language*, 289

[79] Fisher, *The Emergence of Standard English*, 14-15

[80] Freeman, *Conquest of England, vol. V*, 54

# Illustrations

Inside Cover Photo: Monument to William the Conqueror at Falaise/Picryl Stock Photo

1. Roman Britain: Great Witcombe Roman villa, circa A.D. 250. Ivan Lapper/Alamy Stock Photo
2. The destruction of Roman Britain/Alamy Stock Photo
3. Costumes of the world: Anglo-Saxons/Picryl Stock Photo
4. Augustine preaching before King Ethelbert. James W. E. Doyle/Picryl Stock Photo
5. Viking Armada. Edward Moran/Picryl Stock Photo
6. The Viking sails grew to be dreaded/Picryl Stock Photo
7. A map depicting Britain in the year 886/Picryl Stock Photo
8. Alfred found much pleasure in reading/Picryl Stock Photo
9. Queen Wealhtheaow pledges Beowulf. C.T. Tobin/Picryl Stock Photo
10. Siegfried and Beowulf. G.T. Tobin/Picryl Stock Photo
11. Harold Godwinson. *Chronicle*/Alamy Stock Photo
12. William I. The Print Collector/Alamy Stock Photo
13. William the Conqueror arriving in England/Look and Learn Stock Photo
14. Harold and Edith statue. C.A.W.Wilke/Picryl Stock Photo
15. A view of the Tower of London from across the street/Picryl Stock Photo
16. Windsor Castle/Picryl Stock Photo
17. Westminster Abby/ Picryl Stock Photo

18. Coronation of William I after his conquest of England, 1066. North Wind Picture Archives/Alamy Stock Photo
19. Costumes of all Nations: Norman/Picryl Stock Photo
20. Depopulation of Hampshire to form the New Forest/ Picryl Stock Photo
21. Vineyard, vines/Picryl Stock Photo
22. Richard the Lionhearted. Merry-Joseph Blondel/Picryl Stock Photo
23. Bold Robin Hood and his outlaw band. Louis Rhead/Picryl Stock Photo
24. Anglo-French life: Tristan and Isolde. Edmund Leighton/ Picryl Stock Photo
25. (Anglo-Saxon) Poverty/USA Public Domain
26. St. Louis mediating between the King of England and his barons/Picryl Stock Photo
27. Reinforcements for the Duke of Brittany, 100 Year's War. British Library/Alamy Stock Photo
28. Edward the Black Prince presenting King John of France to his father. *Cassell's Illustrated History of England, Vol. I*/Picryl Stock Photo
29. The Black Death XV-A painting of a man in a bed/Picryl Stock Photo
30. Richard II takes control of the rebels. *A Chronicle of England*/Picryl Stock Photo
31. *Canterbury Tales*, detail of mural, North Reading Room. Ezra Winter. Library of Congress/Picryl Stock Photo
32. Meeting of Richard and Henry /*A Chronicle of England*, page 338, /Picryl Stock Photo

33. Henry V at Agincourt/Picryl Stock Photo
34. Henry V weds Katherine of France. *A Chronicle of England*/Picryl Stock Photo
35. Jeanne d'Arc. Henri Chapu/Picryl Stock Photo
36. Jean Miélot at his desk/Picryl Stock Photo
37. Caxton showing specimens of his printing to King Edward IV and his Queen. *The Graphic* 1877/Picryl Stock Photo
38. Field of Cloth of Gold/Picryl Stock Photo
39. King Henry VIII. National Portrait Gallery/Picryl Stock Photo
40. Anne Boleyn. National Trust/Picryl Stock Photo
41. Cobbe portrait of William Shakespeare. Walters Art Museum/Picryl Stock Photo
42. *Twelfth Night*: TCD. Prod.DB/Alamy Stock Photo
43. Rochester and Jane Eyre. Frederick Walker, A.R.A./USA Public Domain
44. British passport 2020/Picryl Stock Photo

## About the Author

As a student at Swarthmore College, Carol Williams Kisch was planning a career as a mathematics instructor until, on the day that she was offered an opportunity to study closely with Roland Barthes and Jean-Louis Ferrier in Paris, she abruptly changed her major to French literature. After graduation, she taught English at L'École Nationale d'Administration in Ouagadougou, Burkino Faso for three years and then worked as a translator for USAID in Bamako, Mali, before moving back to Paris where she gave English lessons for future diplomats at L'É.N.A. and worked on more translations. After returning to California, she earned her master's degree from Claremont Graduate University. For 38 years, she taught English classes for foreign students at the University of California and language teaching methodology classes, both on the UC campus and as intensive UC courses in Argentina, Taiwan, Japan, and Korea. Carol Williams Kisch officially retired in 2016 but continued to teach an academic writing workshop for foreign graduate students and an occasional writing class at a local language school. She retired completely in 2022, after teaching the English language for 50 years.

Ms. Williams Kisch is happy to meet, either in-person or remotely, as her schedule permits, with groups of readers who share her interest in the topics raised in this book. Please address all inquiries to: info@althofpress.com.

# NOTES

# NOTES

# NOTES

www.ingramcontent.com/pod-product-compliance
Lightning Source LLC
Chambersburg PA
CBHW050520100526
44581CB00002B/51